Cite Right

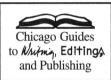

Chicago Guides
to *Writing*, Editing*s*
and Publishing

Cite Right

A Quick Guide to Citation Styles — MLA, APA, Chicago, the Sciences, Professions, and More

Charles Lipson

The University of Chicago Press CHICAGO AND LONDON

The University of Chicago Press, Chicago 60637

The University of Chicago Press, Ltd., London

Published 2018

Printed in the United States of America

27 26 25 24 23 22 21   4 5

ISBN-13: 978-0-226-43110-9 (paper)

ISBN-13: 978-0-226-43124-6 (e-book)

DOI: https://doi.org/10.7208/chicago/9780226431246.001.0001

Library of Congress Cataloging-in-Publication Data

Names: Lipson, Charles, author.

Title: Cite right : a quick guide to citation styles—MLA, APA, Chicago, the sciences, professions, and more / Charles Lipson.

Other titles: Chicago guides to writing, editing, and publishing.

Description: Third edition. | Chicago ; London : The University of Chicago Press, 2018. | Series: Chicago guides to writing, editing, and publishing | Includes index.

Identifiers: LCCN 2018021877 | ISBN 9780226431109 (pbk. : alk. paper) | ISBN 9780226431246 (e-book)

Subjects: LCSH: Bibliographical citations.

Classification: LCC PN171.F56 L55 2018 | DDC 808.02/7—dc23

LC record available at https://lccn.loc.gov/2018021877

To my students,

who have made

teaching so rewarding

CONTENTS

Citations: An Overview

1 WHY CITE?

There are three reasons to cite the materials you use:

- To give credit to others' work and ideas, whether you agree with them or not. When you use their words, you must give them credit by using both quotation marks and citations.
- To show readers the materials on which you base your analysis, your narrative, or your conclusions.
- To guide readers to the materials you have used so they can examine them for themselves. Their interest might be to confirm your work, to challenge it, or simply to explore it further.

Taken together, these citations fully disclose your sources. That's important for academic integrity in several ways.

First, good citations parcel out credit. Some belongs to you for the original work you did; you need to take full responsibility for it. Some belongs to others for their words, ideas, data, drawings, or other work; you need to acknowledge it, openly and explicitly.

Second, if you relied on others' work in order to tell your story, explain your topic, or document your conclusions, you need to say exactly what you used. Take a sample paper about World War I. No one writing today learned about it firsthand. What we know, we learned by reading books and articles, by examining original documents and news reports, by listening to oral histories, by reviewing data compiled by military historians, and perhaps by viewing photographs or movies. When we write about the war, then, we should say how we acquired our information. The only exception is "commonly known information," facts that everyone in the field clearly understands and that do not require any substantiation.[1] There's no need for a footnote to prove Woodrow Wilson was actually president of the United States. But if you referred to his speech declaring war, you would need a proper citation. If you used his words, you'd need quotation marks too.

---

1. What counts as common knowledge depends on your audience.

Third, your readers may want to pursue a particular issue you covered. Citations should lead them to the right sources, whether those are books, interviews, archival documents, websites, poems, or paintings. That guidance serves several purposes. Skeptical readers may doubt the basis for your work or your conclusions. Others may simply want to double-check them or do more research on the topic. Your citations should point the way.

What citations should *not* do is prance about showing off your knowledge without adding to the reader's. That's just bragging.

Beyond this question of style (and good manners), there is the basic issue of honesty. *Citations should never mislead your readers.* There are lots of ways to mislead or misdirect your readers; accurate citations avoid them. For example, they should not imply you read books or articles when you really didn't. They should not imply you spent days in the archives deciphering original documents when you actually read them in an edited book or, worse, when you "borrowed" the citation from a scholar who *did* study the originals. Of course it's fine to cite that author or an edited collection. That's accurate. It's fine to burrow into the archives and read the original yourself. It's dishonest, though, to write citations that only pretend you did.

Good citations should reveal your sources, not conceal them. They should honestly show the research you conducted. That means they should give credit where credit is due, disclose the materials on which you base your work, and guide readers to that material so they can explore it further. Citations like those accurately reflect your work and that of others. They show the ground on which you stand.

WHICH CITATION FORMAT SHOULD YOU USE?

With so many formats available, which one should you choose?

The answer is usually straightforward: most fields rely on one format. In English literature, for instance, most papers and articles use MLA. In chemistry they use ACS. A few fields, such as engineering, use more than one style, depending on the journal or publisher. Political science also uses two styles: APA for journals that prefer in-text citations and Chicago for journals that prefer true footnotes or endnotes. All these styles, and many more, are included in the chapters that follow.

Cite Right labels each chapter so you can see which fields use which style. If you are still unsure, you can find the answer in a couple of ways. If you're a student, simply ask your professor or teaching assistant. If you're writing for publication in a journal, review that journal's recent articles and its instructions for authors, either in the journal itself or on its website. Even if you don't plan on getting published, it's a good idea to look at the leading journals in your field and follow their style.

2 THE BASICS OF CITATION

Acknowledging your sources is crucial to doing honest academic work. That means citing them properly, using one of several styles. The one you choose depends on your field, your professor's advice if you are a student, and your own preferences.

There are three major citation styles:

- Chicago (or Turabian), used in many fields
- MLA, used in the humanities
- APA, used in social sciences, education, and business

Several sciences have also developed their own distinctive styles:

- CSE for the biological sciences
- AMA for the biomedical sciences, medicine, nursing, and dentistry
- ACS for chemistry
- AIP for physics, plus other styles for astrophysics and astronomy
- various styles for mathematics, computer sciences, and engineering

I will cover each one, providing clear directions and plenty of examples so you won't have any trouble writing correct citations. That way you can concentrate on your paper, not on the type of citation you're using. I'll cover each style separately so you can turn directly to the one you need. Using this information, you'll be able to cite books, articles, websites, films, musical performances, government documents, text messages, podcasts, tweets—whatever you use in your papers.

Why would you ever want to use different citation styles? Why can't you just pick one and stick with it? Because different fields won't let you. They have designed citation styles to meet their special needs, whether it's genetics or German, and you'll just have to use the appropriate one. In some sciences, for instance, proper citations list only the author, journal, and pages. They omit the article's title. If you did that in the humanities or social sciences, you'd be incorrect because proper citations for those fields *require* the title. Go figure.

Compare these bibliographic citations for an article of mine:

Chicago	Lipson. Charles. "Why Are Some International Agreements Informal?" *International Organization* 45, no. 4 (Autumn 1991): 495–538.
APA	Lipson, C. (1991). Why are some international agreements informal? *International Organization*, 45, 495–538.
ACS	Lipson, C. *Int. Org.* 1991, 45, 495.

None of these is complicated, but they *are* different. When you leave the chemistry lab to take a course on Shakespeare, you'll leave behind your citation style as well as your beakers. Not to worry. For chemistry papers, just turn to chapter 8. For Shakespeare, turn to chapter 4, which covers MLA citations for the humanities. Both chapters include lots of examples, presented in simple tables, so it won't be "double, double toil and trouble."

Despite their differences, *all these citation styles have the same basic goals*:

- to identify and credit the sources you use; and
- to give readers specific information so they can access these sources themselves if they wish.

Fortunately, the different styles include a lot of the same information. That means you can write down the same things as you take notes, without worrying about what kind of citations you will ultimately use. You should write down that information as soon as you start taking notes on a new source. If you print out, photocopy, or download an article, write all the reference information on the first page. If you do it immediately, you won't forget. You'll need it later for citations.

Or maybe you will be working with an online citation generator. These programs can do a lot of the work of gathering and formatting the information for you. But some of them are better and more reliable than others. Some can handle only the most common citation styles or source types (good luck if you need to cite a podcast in CSE style!). It's your responsibility to make sure your citations are accurate and complete, and this book can help you get the details right for a wide range of styles and sources.

How these citations will ultimately look depends on which style you use. Most styles include some kind of marker in the text, immediately following the material you need to cite, and a fuller listing of the details of the source elsewhere in the paper, usually at the end. The in-text marker might be a number, given as a superscript [99] or in brackets [99] or parentheses (99). Or it might be a note in parentheses including a couple of key pieces of the citation, such as the author's last name plus the publication date or page number. The fuller listing usually includes the author's name, the title of the source, the publication date, and other details.

For example, Chicago (or Turabian)[1] style uses notes keyed to superscript numbers in the text. You place the notes either at the bottom of each page (footnotes) or at the end of the document (endnotes). Footnotes and endnotes are identical, except for their placement. Word processors give you an easy choice between the two. The notes contain either complete citations or shortened versions, plus a bibliography at the end of the paper.

The other two major citation styles—MLA and APA[2]—look a little different. They use in-text citations such as (Stewart 154) or (Stewart, 2018) with full information provided only in a reference list at the end.[3]

Your department, school, or publisher may prefer one style or even require it, or they might leave it up to you. Check on that as soon as you begin writing papers with citations. Why not do it consistently from the beginning?

> *Tip on selecting a citation style*: Check with your teachers in each class to find out what style citations they prefer. Then use that style consistently.

Speaking of consistency, it's important for proper citations. Stick with the same abbreviations and capitalizations, and don't mix styles within a paper. It's easy to write "Volume" in one citation, "Vol." in another, and

---

1. As explained in chapter 3, these two names refer to the same style, as covered in two different books published by the University of Chicago Press. *The Chicago Manual of Style*, 17th ed. (Chicago: University of Chicago Press, 2017) is the most comprehensive treatment of the style. Students can find everything they need in a separate book, Kate L. Turabian, *A Manual for Writers of Research Papers, Theses, and Dissertations*, 9th ed., rev. Wayne C. Booth, Gregory C. Colomb, Joseph M. Williams, Joseph Bizup, William T. FitzGerald, and the University of Chicago Press Editorial Staff (Chicago: University of Chicago Press, 2018).

2. In case you are wondering about the initials: MLA stands for the Modern Language Association and APA stands for the American Psychological Association. See chapters 4 and 5 for more details.

3. Reference lists are similar to bibliographies, but there are some technical differences. In later chapters I'll explain the details (and nomenclature) of each style.

"vol." in a third. We all do it, and then we have to correct it. We all abbreviate "chapter" as both "chap." and "ch." Just try your best the first time around, and then go back and fix the mistakes when you revise. That's why they invented the search-and-replace function.

My goal here is to provide a one-stop reference so that you can handle nearly all citation issues you'll face, regardless of which style you use and what kinds of items you cite. For each style, I'll show you how to cite books, articles, unpublished papers, websites, and lots more. For specialized documents such as musical scores or scientific preprints, I show citations only in the fields that actually use them. Physicists often cite preprints, but they don't cite Beethoven. The physics chapter reflects those needs. Students in the humanities not only cite Beethoven; they cite dance performances, plays, and poems. I have included MLA citations for all of them. In case you need to cite something well off the beaten path, I'll explain where to find additional information for each style.

HANGING INDENTS

One final point about shared bibliographic style. Most bibliographies and reference lists—Chicago, MLA, APA, and some of the sciences—use a special style known as "hanging indents." This applies only to the bibliography and not to footnotes or endnotes. It is the opposite of regular paragraph indention, where the first line is indented and the rest are regular length. In a hanging indent, the first line of each citation is regular length and the rest are indented. For example:

Rothenberg, Gunther E. "Maurice of Nassau, Gustavus Adolphus, Raimondo Montecuccoli, and the 'Military Revolution' of the Seventeenth Century." In *Makers of Modern Strategy from Machiavelli to the Nuclear Age*, edited by Peter Paret, 32–63. Princeton, NJ: Princeton University Press, 1986.

Spooner, Frank C. *Risks at Sea: Amsterdam Insurance and Maritime Europe, 1766–1780*. Cambridge: Cambridge University Press, 1983.

There's a good reason for this unusual format. Hanging indents are designed to make it easy to skim down the list of references and see the authors' names. To remind you to use this format, I'll use it myself when I illustrate references in the citation styles that use it. (The only ones that don't use hanging indents are science styles with numbered citations. It's actually not complicated, and I'll explain it later.)

To make the authors' names stand out further, most bibliographies or reference lists put their last names first. If an author's name is repeated, however, the styles differ. APA repeats the full name for each citation. Chicago used to call for three em dashes (that is, long dashes), followed by a period, but now encourages repeating the author's name, like APA.[4] MLA uses three hyphens followed by a period.

> Talbot, Ian. *A History of Modern South Asia: Politics, States, Diasporas.* Yale UP, 2016.
> ---. *Pakistan: A Modern History.* Palgrave Macmillan, 2010.

You can arrange hanging indents easily on your word processor. Go to the format feature and, within it, the section on paragraphs. Choose hanging indentation instead of regular or none.

WHERE TO FIND MORE

So far I have covered some basic issues that apply to most citation styles. There are, of course, lots more questions, some that apply to all styles and some that apply only to one or two. Rather than cover these questions now, I'll handle them in the chapters on individual citation styles and in a final chapter on frequently asked questions (FAQs).

If you have questions that aren't covered in the chapter on your citation style, be sure to check the FAQs chapter. If you still have questions, you can always go to the reference book for a given style. Most styles have them (but not all). I'll list them in the chapters for individual styles.

ON TO THE NUTS AND BOLTS

I have organized the references so they are most convenient for you, putting all the documentation for each style in its own chapter.

> Chapter 3: Chicago (or Turabian) citations
> Chapter 4: MLA citations for the humanities

---

4. Because em dashes are longer than hyphens, they show up differently on screen and in print. The em dashes show up as a solid line, the hyphens as separate dashes. Three em dashes: ———. Three hyphens: ---. Frankly, you don't need to worry about this for your papers. Use the preferred one if you can, but either is fine.

Chapter 5: APA citations for the social sciences, education, and business

Chapter 6: CSE citations for the biological sciences

Chapter 7: AMA citations for the biomedical sciences, medicine, nursing, and dentistry

Chapter 8: ACS citations for chemistry

Chapter 9: Physics, astrophysics, and astronomy citations

Chapter 10: Mathematics, computer science, and engineering citations

Within each chapter I've started with some general information about the style covered, and then moved on to examples of how to cite specific kinds of sources. I've put the most common types of sources at the beginning—usually books or journal articles—and grouped similar sources together. For the first three chapters, which are the longest and most detailed, I've also provided an index of the source types early in the chapter. You can use the index to go right to the examples for journal articles or blog posts or whatever you need to cite.

I've included a wide range of online and other electronic sources. In some cases the official style guides don't cover things like podcasts or text messages, either because the field that follows that style doesn't use them as sources or because the style guide hasn't been updated lately. Where I thought you might need to cite a source like this, I have provided examples based on the style's general rules. Since there are new types of sources to cite all the time, you might need to do the same thing if there isn't an example here.

Don't bother trying to memorize any of these styles. There are simply too many minor details. Just follow the tables, and you'll be able to handle different sources—from journal articles to podcasts—in whichever style you need to use. Later, as you write more papers, you'll become familiar with the style you use most.

After explaining each style and answering questions about it, I will also answer some common questions that apply to every style. That's in chapter 11. Now let's see how to do citations and bibliographies in the specific style you want to use.

Citations in Every Format:
A Quick Guide

3 CHICAGO (OR TURABIAN) CITATIONS

Chicago citations are based on the authoritative *Chicago Manual of Style*, published by the University of Chicago Press. The manual, now in its seventeenth edition (2017), is the bible for references and academic style, and is also available online at www.chicagomanualofstyle.org. A briefer version, covering most aspects of student papers, is Kate L. Turabian's *A Manual for Writers of Research Papers, Theses, and Dissertations*, now in its ninth edition (2018). This section, however, should cover all you need to document your sources, even if they're unusual.

FULL NOTES, SHORT NOTES, AND BIBLIOGRAPHY

Chicago-style notes come in two flavors, and I include both in this section.[1]

1. A complete first note + short follow-up notes

The first note for any item is a full one, giving complete information about the book, article, or other document. Subsequent entries for that item are brief. There is no need for a bibliography since all the information is covered in the first note (but your department or publisher may require one, so check with them first).

2. Short notes only + bibliography

All notes are brief. Full information about the sources appears only in the bibliography.

This means there are three ways to cite individual items. All of them are illustrated in this chapter.

---

1. *The Chicago Manual of Style* and Turabian also describe another style, the author-date system. These citations appear in parentheses in the text, listing the author and the date of publication. For example: (Walls 2017). Full citations appear in a reference list at the end. For simplicity, I have omitted this style since it is similar to APA, discussed in chapter 5.

A. Full first notes
B. Short notes
C. Bibliographic entries

The first flavor combines A + B, the second combines B + C.

This chapter covers everything from edited books to online journals, from sheet music to music videos, and lots of things in between. To make it easy to find what you need, I've listed them here alphabetically, together with the pages they are on. At the end of this chapter I answer some questions about using this style.

INDEX OF CHICAGO CITATIONS IN THIS CHAPTER

CHICAGO MANUAL OF STYLE: NOTES AND BIBLIOGRAPHY

Book, one author	Full first note	[99] Charles Lipson, *Reliable Partners: How Democracies Have Made a Separate Peace* (Princeton, NJ: Princeton University Press, 2003), 22–23.

> ▸ This is note number 99 and refers to pages 22–23.
> ▸ Footnotes and endnotes do not have hanging indents. Only the bibliography does.

[99] Terry McDermott, *Off Speed: Baseball, Pitching, and the Art of Deception* (New York: Pantheon, 2017), 1028.

> ▸ Chicago abbreviates consecutive page numbers as follows: if the first number is two digits or less, repeat all digits (1–12, 44–68); if the first number is three digits or more and not a multiple of one hundred, include only the changed part (203–6, 345–52, 349–402 *but* 200–223). If this sounds confusing, it is. Fortunately, it's always acceptable to repeat all digits.

Short note

[99] Lipson, *Reliable Partners*, 22–23.
[99] McDermott, *Off Speed*, 102–8.

> ▸ Shorten titles to four words or fewer, if possible.

Bibliography

Lipson, Charles. *Reliable Partners: How Democracies Have Made a Separate Peace.* Princeton, NJ: Princeton University Press, 2003.

McDermott, Terry. *Off Speed: Baseball, Pitching, and the Art of Deception.* New York: Pantheon, 2017.

Books, several by same author	First note	[99] Ian Talbot, *A History of Modern South Asia: Politics, States, Diasporas* (New Haven, CT: Yale University Press, 2016). [100] Ian Talbot, *Pakistan: A Modern History* (London: Palgrave Macmillan, 2010).
	Short note	[99] Talbot, *History of Modern South Asia*. [100] Talbot, *Pakistan*.

| Books, several by same author (*continued*) | Bibliography | Talbot, Ian. *A History of Modern South Asia: Politics, States, Diasporas*. New Haven, CT: Yale University Press, 2016. |
| | | Talbot, Ian. *Pakistan: A Modern History*. London: Palgrave Macmillan, 2010. |

▸ For multiple books by the same author, simply repeat the author's name in the bibliography. You may instead use three em dashes (which are simply long dashes), followed by a period, but this method is not recommended because it may obscure important information in the entry. If you're not sure how to create the em dash, just use three hyphens.

▸ List works for each author alphabetically by title. In alphabetizing, disregard any initial article: *A, An, The*.

| Book, multiple authors | First note | [99] John Martin Fischer and Benjamin Mitchell-Yellin, *Near-Death Experiences: Understanding Visions of the Afterlife* (Oxford: Oxford University Press, 2016), 15–18. |

▸ For four or more authors, use only the first author's name plus "et al." (Latin *et alii*, "and others"). For example, if this one had four-plus authors: John Martin Fischer et al., *Near-Death* . . .

| | Short note | [99] Fischer and Mitchell-Yellin, *Near-Death Experiences*, 15–18. |

▸ Titles with four words or fewer are not shortened.

| | Bibliography | Fischer, John Martin, and Benjamin Mitchell-Yellin. *Near-Death Experiences: Understanding Visions of the Afterlife*. Oxford: Oxford University Press, 2016. |

▸ Only the first author's name is inverted.

▸ List up to ten coauthors in the bibliography. If there are more, list the first seven, followed by "et al."

| Book, multiple editions | First note | [99] Annelise Orleck, *Common Sense and a Little Fire: Women and Working-Class Politics in the United States, 1900–1965*, 2nd ed. (Chapel Hill: University of North Carolina Press, 2017). |

[99] William Strunk Jr. and E. B. White, *The Elements of Style*, 50th anniversary ed. (New York: Longman, 2009), 12.

Short note

[99] Orleck, *Common Sense.*
[99] Strunk and White, *Elements of Style*, 12.
▶ To keep the note short, the title doesn't include the initial article (*The Elements of Style*) or the edition number.

Bibliography

Orleck, Annelise. *Common Sense and a Little Fire: Women and Working-Class Politics in the United States, 1900–1965*, 2nd ed. Chapel Hill: University of North Carolina Press, 2017.
Strunk, William, Jr., and E. B. White. *The Elements of Style*. 50th anniversary ed. New York: Longman, 2009.

Book, edited

First note

[99] Annie Bunting and Joel Quirk, eds., *Contemporary Slavery: Popular Rhetoric and Political Practice* (Vancouver: University of British Columbia Press, 2017).
[99] Jeffrey Ian Ross, ed., *Routledge Handbook of Graffiti and Street Art* (New York: Routledge, 2016).
[99] Mirjam Künkler, John Madeley, and Shylashri Shankar, eds., *A Secular Age beyond the West* (Cambridge: Cambridge University Press, 2017).

Short note

[99] Bunting and Quirk, *Contemporary Slavery.*
▶ Do not include the abbreviation for editor in short notes.
[99] Ross, *Graffiti and Street Art.*
▶ Choose the most relevant words when shortening the title.
[99] Künkler, Madeley, and Shankar, *Secular Age.*

Bibliography

Bunting, Annie, and Joel Quirk, eds. *Contemporary Slavery: Popular Rhetoric and Political Practice*. Vancouver: University of British Columbia Press, 2017.

Book, edited (*continued*)		Ross, Jeffrey Ian, ed. *Routledge Handbook of Graffiti and Street Art*. New York: Routledge, 2016. Künkler, Mirjam, John Madeley, and Shylashri Shankar, eds. *A Secular Age beyond the West*. Cambridge: Cambridge University Press, 2017.
Book, anonymous or no author	First note	[99] Anonymous, *The Secret Lives of Teachers* (Chicago: University of Chicago Press, 2015). [99] *Golden Verses of the Pythagoreans* (Whitefish, MT: Kessinger, 2003).
	Short note	[99] Anonymous, *Secret Lives of Teachers*. [99] *Golden Verses of Pythagoreans*.
	Bibliography	Anonymous. *The Secret Lives of Teachers*. Chicago: University of Chicago Press, 2015. *Golden Verses of the Pythagoreans*. Whitefish, MT: Kessinger, 2003. ▸ If a book lists "anonymous" as the author, then that word should be included. If no author is listed, then you may list "anonymous" or simply begin with the title.
E-book	First note	[99] Gary Taubes, *The Case against Sugar* (New York: Alfred A. Knopf, 2016), Kindle. [99] Kate Auspitz, *Wallis's War: A Novel of Diplomacy and Intrigue* (Chicago: University of Chicago Press, 2015), iBooks. ▸ For e-books, include the name of the device or app used to read the book. If a file format such as EPUB or PDF is specified, you can note that in addition to the name of the device or app (e.g., Adobe Digital Editions EPUB). ▸ To specify location within an e-book, it's best to cite a chapter number, section heading, or other signpost, since page and location numbers may vary depending on the device or app.
	Short note	[99] Taubes, *Case against Sugar*, chap. 2. [99] Auspitz, *Wallis's War*.
	Bibliography	Taubes, Gary. *The Case against Sugar*. New York: Alfred A. Knopf, 2016. Kindle.

Auspitz, Kate. *Wallis's War: A Novel of Diplo-
macy and Intrigue.* Chicago: University of
Chicago Press, 2015. iBooks. Adobe Digital
Editions EPUB.

Book, online	First note	[99] Charles Dickens, *Great Expectations* (1867; Project Gutenberg, 2008), chap. 2, http://www.gutenberg.org/files/1400/1400-h/1400-h.htm. [99] Frederick Jackson Turner, *The Frontier in American History* (New York: Henry Holt, 1921), 6, https://books.google.com/books/about/The_Frontier_in_American_History.html?id=vtF1AAAAMAAJ. ▸ Include the URL as the last part of the citation. A URL based on a DOI (appended to https://doi.org/) is preferable to a URL. ▸ There are often multiple formats of a book available online. When possible, use scanned pages of a printed book instead of reflowable text (like HTML or EPUB). It is more authoritative and will make page citation easier. The Turner edition here is a scanned version of the original. ▸ If you can't find a version with page numbers, refer to a chapter number, section heading, or similar signpost.
	Short note	[99] Dickens, *Great Expectations*, chap. 2. [99] Turner, *Frontier in American History*, 6.
	Bibliography	Dickens, Charles. *Great Expectations.* 1867. Project Gutenberg, 2008.http://www.gutenberg.org/files/1400/1400-h/1400-h.htm. Turner, Frederick Jackson. *The Frontier in American History.* New York: Henry Holt, 1921. https://books.google.com/books/about/The_Frontier_in_American_History.html?id=vtF1AAAAMAAJ.

Multivolume work	First note	[99] Otto Pflanze, *Bismarck and the Development of Germany*, 3 vols. (Princeton, NJ: Princeton University Press, 1963–90), 1:153.

Multivolume work (*continued*)		[99] Babette Rothschild, *The Body Remembers*, 2 vols. (New York: W. W. Norton, 2017), 2:16.
	Short note	[99] Pflanze, *Bismarck*, 1:153. [99] Rothschild, *Body Remembers*, 2:16.
	Bibliography	Pflanze, Otto. *Bismarck and the Development of Germany.* 3 vols. Princeton, NJ: Princeton University Press, 1963–90. Rothschild, Babette. *The Body Remembers*, 2 vols. New York: W. W. Norton, 2017.
Single volume in a multivolume work	First note	[99] Robert A. Caro, *The Years of Lyndon Johnson*, vol. 4, *The Passage of Power* (New York: Alfred A. Knopf, 2012), 237. [99] Bruce E. Johansen, *Global Warming in the 21st Century*, vol. 2, *Melting Ice and Warming Seas* (Westport, CT: Praeger, 2006), 71. [99] Akira Iriye, *The Globalizing of America*, vol. 3 of *Cambridge History of American Foreign Relations*, ed. Warren I. Cohen (Cambridge: Cambridge University Press, 1993), 124. ▸ Caro wrote all three volumes. Iriye wrote only the third volume in a series edited by Cohen.
	Short note	[99] Caro, *Years of Lyndon Johnson*, 4:237. ▸ or [99] Caro, *Passage of Power*, 237. [99] Johansen, *Global Warming*, 2:71. ▸ or [99] Johansen, *Melting Ice and Warming Seas*, 71. [99] Iriye, *Globalizing of America*, 124.
	Bibliography	Caro, Robert A. *The Years of Lyndon Johnson.* Vol. 4, *The Passage of Power.* New York: Alfred A. Knopf, 2012. Johansen, Bruce E. *Global Warming in the 21st Century.* Vol. 2, *Melting Ice and Warming Seas.* Westport, CT: Praeger, 2006. Iriye, Akira. *The Globalizing of America.* Vol. 3 of *Cambridge History of American Foreign Relations*, edited by Warren I. Cohen. Cambridge: Cambridge University Press, 1993.

Reprint of earlier edition	First note	[99] Jacques Barzun, *Simple and Direct: A Rhetoric for Writers*, rev. ed. (1985; repr., Chicago: University of Chicago Press, 1994), 27. [99] Adam Smith, *An Inquiry into the Nature and Causes of the Wealth of Nations* (1776), ed. Edwin Cannan (Chicago: University of Chicago Press, 1976). ▸ The year 1776 appears immediately after the title because that's when Smith's original work appeared. The editor, Edwin Cannan, worked only on its modern publication. The Barzun volume, by contrast, is simply a reprint so the original year appears as part of the publication information.
	Short note	[99] Barzun, *Simple and Direct*, 27. [99] Smith, *Wealth of Nations*, vol. I, bk. IV, chap. II: 477. ▸ This modern edition of Smith is actually a single volume, but it retains the volume numbering of the 1776 original. You could simply cite the page number, but the full citation helps readers with other editions.
	Bibliography	Barzun, Jacques. *Simple and Direct: A Rhetoric for Writers*. 1985. Reprint, Chicago: University of Chicago Press, 1994. Smith, Adam. *An Inquiry into the Nature and Causes of the Wealth of Nations*. 1776. Edited by Edwin Cannan. Chicago: University of Chicago Press, 1976.
Translated volume	First note	[99] Hesiod, *The Poems of Hesiod: Theogony, Works and Days, & The Shield of Herakles*, trans. Barry B. Powell (Oakland: University of California Press, 2017), 30–35. [99] Alexis de Tocqueville, *Democracy in America* (1835), ed. J. P. Mayer, trans. George Lawrence (New York: HarperCollins, 2000). ▸ Translator and editor are listed in the order they appear on the book's title page. [99] Seamus Heaney, trans., *Beowulf: A New Verse Translation* (New York: Farrar, Straus and Giroux, 2000).

Translated
volume
(*continued*)

▶ For *Beowulf*, the translator's name appears before the book title because Heaney's is the only name on the title page. (The poem is anonymous.) The same treatment would be given to an editor or compiler whose name appeared alone on the title page.

Short note

[99] Hessiod, *Poems*, 30–35.
[99] Tocqueville, *Democracy in America*.
[99] *Beowulf*.
▶ or
[99] Heaney, *Beowulf*.

Bibliography

Hesiod. *The Poems of Hesiod: Theogony, Works and Days, & The Shield of Herakles*. Translated by Barry B. Powell. Oakland: University of California Press, 2017.

Tocqueville, Alexis de. *Democracy in America*. 1835. Edited by J. P. Mayer. Translated by George Lawrence. New York: HarperCollins, 2000.

Heaney, Seamus, trans. *Beowulf: A New Verse Translation*. New York: Farrar, Straus and Giroux, 2000.

Chapter in
edited book

First note

[99] Benjamin J. Cohen, "The Macrofoundations of Monetary Power," in *International Monetary Power*, ed. David M. Andrews (Ithaca, NY: Cornell University Press, 2006), 31–50.

Short note

[99] Cohen, "The Macrofoundations of Monetary Power," 31–50.

Bibliography

Cohen, Benjamin J. "The Macrofoundations of Monetary Power." In *International Monetary Power*, edited by David M. Andrews, 31–50. Ithaca, NY: Cornell University Press, 2006.

Journal article

First note

[99] Stefan Timmermans, "Matching Genotype and Phenotype: A Pragmatist Semiotic Analysis of Clinical Exome Sequencing," *American Journal of Sociology* 123, no. 1 (July 2017): 137.

[99] Smita Sahgal, "Situating Kingship within an Embryonic Frame of Masculinity in Early India," *Social Scientist* 43, no. 11/12 (November–December 2015): 5, http://www .jstor.org.pnw.idm.oclc.org/stable/24642382.
[99] Krista A. Capps, Carla L. Atkinson, and Amanda T. Rugenski, "Implications of Species Addition and Decline for Nutrient Dynamics in Fresh Waters," *Freshwater Science* 34, no. 2 (June 2015): 490, https://doi.org/10.1086/ 681095.

- For journal articles accessed online, include the URL or Digital Object Identifier (DOI) as the last part of the citation. A URL based on a DOI (appended to https://doi.org/) is preferable to another type of URL. If there is no DOI or URL, list the name of the database.
- For four or more authors, list only the first author's name plus "et al."
- Cite an abstract the same way you would a journal article, but add the word *abstract* after the article title.

Short note

[99] Timmermans, "Matching Genotype and Phenotype," 137.
[99] Sahgal, "Situating Kingship," 5.
[99] Capps, Atkinson, and Rugenski, "Implications of Species Addition and Decline," 490.

- In a note, refer only to the page(s) cited, if any; in a bibliography, give the page range for the whole article.

Bibliography

Timmermans, Stefan. "Matching Genotype and Phenotype: A Pragmatist Semiotic Analysis of Clinical Exome Sequencing." *American Journal of Sociology* 123, no. 1 (July 2017): 137–77.
Sahgal, Smita. "Situating Kingship within an Embryonic Frame of Masculinity in Early India." *Social Scientist* 43, no. 11/12 (November–December 2015): 3–26. http:// www.jstor.org.pnw.idm.oclc.org/stable/ 24642382.

Journal article (*continued*)		Capps, Krista A., Carla L. Atkinson, and Amanda T. Rugenski. "Implications of Species Addition and Decline for Nutrient Dynamics in Fresh Waters." *Freshwater Science* 34, no. 2 (June 2015): 485–96, https://doi.org/10.1086/681095. ▸ Only the first author's name is inverted. ▸ List up to ten coauthors in the bibliography. If there are more, list the first seven, followed by "et al."
Journal article, foreign language	First note	⁹⁹ Zvi Uri Ma'oz, "Y a-t-il des juifs sans synagogue?," *Revue des Études Juives* 163 (juillet–décembre 2004): 485. ▸ or ⁹⁹ Zvi Uri Ma'oz, "Y a-t-il des juifs sans synagogue?" [Are there Jews without a synagogue?], *Revue des Études Juives* 163 (juillet–décembre 2004): 485.
	Short note	⁹⁹ Ma'oz, "Y a-t-il des juifs sans synagogue?," 485.
	Bibliography	Ma'oz, Zvi Uri. "Y a-t-il des juifs sans synagogue?" *Revue des Études Juives* 163 (juillet–décembre 2004): 483–93. ▸ or Ma'oz, Zvi Uri. "Y a-t-il des juifs sans synagogue?" [Are there Jews without a synagogue?]. *Revue des Études Juives* 163 (juillet–décembre 2004): 483–93.
Newspaper or magazine article	First note	⁹⁹ "Retired U.S. General Is Focus of Inquiry over Iran Leak," *New York Times*, June 28, 2013, A18. ▸ This refers to page A18. You may omit page numbers if you wish, since many newspapers have different editions with different pagination. ⁹⁹ Shivani Vora, "Why Your Airline Says It's Sorry," *New York Times*, July 30, 2017, Sunday edition.

⁹⁹ Evan Halper, "Congress Takes Aim at the Clean Air Act, Putting the Limits of California's Power to the Test," *Los Angeles Times*, August 3, 2017, 3:00 a.m. PDT, http://www.latimes.com/politics/la-na-pol-smog-republicans-20170803-story.html.

▸ Include the URL or DOI at the end of the citation for articles accessed online.

▸ If the article is updated often, include a time stamp as posted with the article.

⁹⁹ Ian Parker, "The Greek Warrior: How a Radical Finance Minister Took on Europe — and Failed," *New Yorker*, August 3, 2015, 46.

▸ Articles in magazines intended for general audiences are treated the same as newspaper articles and cited by date only. Some magazines are more like journals. If you are unsure what you're citing—journal or magazine—look for a volume number. If you spot one without too much trouble, cite as a journal.

Short note

⁹⁹ "Focus of Inquiry," *New York Times*, A18.
⁹⁹ Vora, "Airline Says It's Sorry."
⁹⁹ Harper, "Congress Takes Aim."
⁹⁹ Parker, "The Greek Warrior," 46.

▸ Since newspapers and magazines are usually omitted from the bibliography, use a full citation for the first reference.

Bibliography

▸ Newspaper and magazine articles are left out of bibliographies, but you can include an especially important article:

"Retired U.S. General Is Focus of Inquiry over Iran Leak." *New York Times*. June 28, 2013, A18.

Parker, Ian. "The Greek Warrior: How a Radical Finance Minister Took on Europe — and Failed." *New Yorker*, August 3, 2015, 44–57.

Review   **First note**

⁹⁹ Allison J. Pugh, review of *The Gender Trap: Parents and the Pitfalls of Raising Boys and Girls*, by Emily W. Kane, *American Journal of Sociology* 119, no. 6 (May 2014): 1773–75.

Review		[99] Giovanni Vimercati, "Soviet Pseudoscience:
(*continued*)		The History of Mind Control," review of *Homo*
		Sovieticus: Brain Waves, Mind Control, and
		Telepathic Destiny, by Wladimir Velminski, *Los*
		Angeles Review of Books, August 20, 2017,
		https://lareviewofbooks.org/article/soviet
		-pseudoscience-the-history-of-mind-control.
	Short note	[99] Pugh, review of *Gender Trap*.
		[99] Vimercati, "Soviet Pseudoscience."
		▶ or
		[99] Vimercati, review of *Homo Sovieticus*.
	Bibliography	Pugh, Allison J. Review of *The Gender Trap:*
		Parents and the Pitfalls of Raising Boys
		and Girls, by Emily W. Kane. *American*
		Journal of Sociology 119, no. 6 (May 2014):
		1773–75.
		Ferguson, Niall. "Ameliorate, Contain, Coerce,
		Destroy." Review of *The Utility of Force:*
		The Art of War in the Modern World, by
		Rupert Smith. *New York Times Book*
		Review, February 4, 2007, 14–15.

Unpublished	First note	[99] Shaojie Tang, "Profit Driven Team Group-
paper, thesis,		ing in Social Networks" (paper presented at
or dissertation		the Thirty-First AAAI Conference on Artificial
		Intelligence, February 4–9, 2017), https://
		aaai.org/ocs/index.php/AAAI/AAAI17/paper/
		view/14791/13741.
		[99] Lance Noble, "One Goal, Multiple Strat-
		egies: Engagement in Sino-American WTO
		Accession Negotiations" (master's thesis,
		University of British Columbia, 2006), 15.
		[99] Luis Manuel Sierra, "Indigenous Neigh-
		borhood Residents in the Urbanization of La
		Paz, Bolivia, 1910–1950," (PhD diss., State
		University of New York at Binghamton, 2013),
		ProQuest.
		▶ If you consult a paper through a commercial
		database, include the name of the database.
		Include a URL for papers consulted online.
	Short note	[99] Tang, "Profit Driven Team Grouping."
		[99] Noble, "One Goal, Multiple Strategies."

[99] Sierra, "Indigenous Neighborhood Residents."

Bibliography   Tang, Shaojie. "Profit Driven Team Grouping in Social Networks." Paper presented at the Thirty-First AAAI Conference on Artificial Intelligence, February 4–9, 2017, https://aaai.org/ocs/index.php/AAAI/AAAI17/paper/view/14791/13741.

Noble, Lance. "One Goal, Multiple Strategies: Engagement in Sino-American WTO Accession Negotiations." Master's thesis, University of British Columbia, 2006.

Sierra, Luis Manuel. "Indigenous Neighborhood Residents in the Urbanization of La Paz, Bolivia, 1910–1950." PhD diss., State University of New York at Binghamton, 2013. ProQuest (3612828).

Preprint or working paper

First note   [99] John C. Rodda et al., "A Comparative Study of the Magnitude, Frequency and Distribution of Intense Rainfall in the United Kingdom," preprint, October 9, 2009, http://precedings.nature.com/documents/3847/version/1.
[99] Daniel P. Gross, "The Ties That Bind: Railroad Gauge Standards and Internal Trade in the 19th Century U.S." (working paper, Berkeley Economic History Lab, University of California, Berkeley, March 2016), http://behl.berkeley.edu/working-papers/.

Short note   [99] Rodda et al., "Rainfall in the United Kingdom."
[99] Gross, "The Ties That Bind."

Bibliography   Rodda, John C., Max A. Little, Harvey J. E. Rodda, and Patrick E. McSharry. "A Comparative Study of the Magnitude, Frequency and Distribution of Intense Rainfall in the United Kingdom." Preprint, October 9, 2009. http://precedings.nature.com/documents/3847/version/1.

Preprint or working paper (*continued*)		Gross, Daniel P. "The Ties That Bind: Railroad Gauge Standards and Internal Trade in the 19th Century U.S." Working paper, Berkeley Economic History Lab, University of California, Berkeley, March 2016. http://behl.berkeley.edu/working-papers/.
Archival materials and manuscript collections, hard copies and online	First note	[99] Isaac Franklin to R. C. Ballard, February 28, 1831, series 1.1, folder 1, Rice Ballard Papers, Southern Historical Collection, Wilson Library, University of North Carolina, Chapel Hill.

▸ Here is the order of items within the citation:
  1. Author and brief description of the item
  2. Date, if possible
  3. Identification number of item or manuscript
  4. Title of the series or collection
  5. Library (or depository) and its location; for well-known libraries and archives, the location may be omitted

[99] Mary Swift Lamson, "An Account of the Beginning of the B.Y.W.C.A.," MS, [n.d.], and accompanying letter, 1891, series I, I-A-2, Boston YWCA Papers, Schlesinger Library, Radcliffe Institute for Advanced Study, Harvard University.

▸ "MS" = manuscript = papers (plural: "MSS")

[99] Sigismundo Taraval, journal recounting Indian uprisings in Baja California [handwritten MS], 1734–37, ¶ 23, Edward E. Ayer Manuscript Collection no. 1240, Newberry Library, Chicago.

▸ This journal has numbered paragraphs. Page numbers, paragraphs, or other identifiers aid readers.

[99] Horatio Nelson Taft, diary, February 20, 1862, p. 149 (vol. 1, January 1, 1861–April 11, 1862), Manuscript Division, Library of Congress, http://memory.loc.gov/ammem/tafthtml/tafthome.html.

[99] Henrietta Szold to Rose Jacobs, February 3, 1932, reel 1, book 1, Rose Jacobs–Alice L. Seligsberg Collection, Judaica Microforms, Brandeis Library, Waltham, MA.

▶ Abbreviations: When a collection's name
and location are often repeated, they may be
abbreviated after the first use:
[99] Henrietta Szold to Rose Jacobs, March 9,
1936, A/125/112, Central Zionist Archives,
Jerusalem (hereafter cited as CZA).
[100] Szold to Eva Stern, July 27, 1936,
A/125/912, CZA.

Short note   [99] Isaac Franklin to R. C. Ballard, February 28,
1831, series 1.1, folder 1, Rice Ballard Papers.
▶ Short-form citation varies for archival items.
The main concerns are readers' convenience
and the proximity of full information in
nearby notes.
[99] Mary Swift Lamson, "Beginning of the
B.Y.W.C.A.," MS [1891], Boston YWCA Papers,
Schlesinger Library.
[99] Sigismundo Taraval, journal recounting
Indian uprisings in Baja California, Edward E.
Ayer Manuscript Collection, Newberry Library.
▶ or
[99] Taraval, journal, Ayer MS Collection, Newberry Library.
[99] Horatio Nelson Taft, diary, February 20,
1862, 149.
[99] Henrietta Szold to Rose Jacobs, February 3,
1932, reel 1, book 1, Rose Jacobs–Alice L.
Seligsberg Collection.
[100] Szold to Jacobs, March 9, 1936, A/125/112,
CZA.
[101] Szold to Eva Stern, July 27, 1936,
A/125/912, CZA.

Bibliography   Rice Ballard Papers. Southern Historical Collection. Wilson Library. University of North
Carolina, Chapel Hill.
▶ In footnotes and endnotes, the specific
archival item is usually listed first because it is
the most important element in the note. For
example: Isaac Franklin to R. C. Ballard, February 28, 1831. In bibliographies, however, the
collection itself is usually listed first because
it is more important. Individual items are not
mentioned in the bibliography *unless* only one
item is cited from a particular collection.

Archival materials and manuscript collections, hard copies and online (*continued*)		Boston YWCA Papers. Schlesinger Library. Radcliffe Institute for Advanced Study, Harvard University. ▸ or Lamson, Mary Swift. "An Account of the Beginning of the B.Y.W.C.A." MS [n.d.] and accompanying letter, 1891. Boston YWCA Papers. Schlesinger Library. Radcliffe Institute for Advanced Study, Harvard University. ▸ If Lamson's account is the only item cited from these papers, then it would be listed in the bibliography. Ayer, Edward E. Manuscript collection. Newberry Library, Chicago, IL. Taft, Horatio Nelson. Diary. Vol. 1, January 1, 1861–April 11, 1862. Manuscript Division, Library of Congress. http://memory.loc.gov/ammem/tafthtml/tafthome.html. Rose Jacobs–Alice L. Seligsberg Collection. Judaica Microforms. Brandeis Library, Waltham, MA. Central Zionist Archives, Jerusalem.
Encyclopedia and dictionary	First note	[99] *Encyclopaedia Britannica*, 15th ed. (1974), s.vv. "Balkans: History," "World War I." [99] *Merriam-Webster*, s.v. "app (n.)," accessed April 6, 2016, http://www.merriam-webster.com/dictionary/app. ▸ The abbreviation s.v. (*sub verbo*) means "under the word." Plural: s.vv. ▸ For print versions you must include the edition but you can omit the publisher, location, and page numbers for well-known references like the *Encyclopaedia Britannica*. [99] *Encyclopaedia Britannica Online*, s.v. "Balkans," accessed September 7, 2016, http://www.britannica.com/EBchecked/topic/50325/Balkans. [99] Dictionary.com, s.v. "metropolitan," accessed August 4, 2017, http://www.dictionary.com/browse/metropolitan?s=t.

▸ Some encyclopedias post a recommended URL alongside each article; use that one instead of the URL that appears in your browser's address bar.

[99] George Graham, "Behaviorism," in *Stanford Encyclopedia of Philosophy*, article published May 26, 2000, revised July 30, 2007, http://plato.stanford.edu/entries/behaviorism/.

▸ or

[99] *Stanford Encyclopedia of Philosophy*, "Behaviorism," by George Graham, article published May 26, 2000, revised July 30, 2007, http://plato.stanford.edu/entries/behaviorism/.

[99] Wikipedia, s.v. "Sufjan Stevens," last modified July 31, 2017, 15:30, https://en.wikipedia.org/wiki/Sufjan_Stevens.

▸ If an article lists a publication date, include it; a last-modified date can be used instead. If neither is available, include an access date.

▸ For reference works with authored entries, you may cite the entry by author, as you would for a contribution to a multiauthored book.

Short note

[99] *Encyclopaedia Britannica*, s.v. "World War I."

[99] *Merriam-Webster's*, s.v. "chronology."

[99] *Encyclopaedia Britannica Online*, s.v. "Balkans."

[99] Dictionary.com, s.v. "metropolitan."

[99] Graham, "Behaviorism."

▸ or

[99] *Stanford Encyclopedia*, "Behaviorism."

[99] Wikipedia, "Sufjan Stevens."

Bibliography

▸ Well-known encyclopedias and dictionaries are not normally listed in bibliographies, but you may wish to include articles from more specialized works, especially if they're authored.

Graham, George. "Behaviorism." In *Stanford Encyclopedia of Philosophy*. Article published May 26, 2000. Revised July 30, 2007. http://plato.stanford.edu/entries/behaviorism/.

Encyclopedia and dictionary (*continued*)		▶ or *Stanford Encyclopedia of Philosophy.* "Behaviorism," by George Graham. Article published May 26, 2000. Revised July 30, 2007. http://plato.stanford.edu/entries/behaviorism/.
Bible, Koran (Qur'an)	First note	[99] Genesis 1:1, 1:3–5, 2:4. [99] Genesis 1:1, 1:3–5, 2:4 (New Revised Standard Version). ▶ Books of the Bible can be abbreviated: Gen. 1:1. ▶ Abbreviations for the next four books are Exod., Lev., Num., and Deut. Abbreviations for other books are easily found with a web search for "abbreviations + Bible." [99] Koran 18:65–82.
	Short note	[99] Genesis 1:1, 1:3–5, 2:4. [99] Koran 18:65–82.
	Bibliography	▶ References to the Bible, Koran, and other sacred texts are not normally included in the bibliography. You may include them, however, if you wish to show that you are using a particular version or translation. Example: Tanakh: The Holy Scriptures: The New JPS Translation according to the Traditional Hebrew Text. Philadelphia: Jewish Publication Society, 1985. ▶ Thou shalt omit the Divine Author's name.
Classical works	First note	▶ Ordinarily, classical Greek and Latin works are referred to in the text itself or in notes. They are not included in the bibliography except to reference the specific translation or commentary by a modern author. Here is an in-text reference: In Pericles' Funeral Oration (2.34–46), Thucydides gives us one of history's most moving speeches. ▶ If you do need to include a note, here is the format: [99] Plato, *The Republic*, trans. R. E. Allen (New Haven, CT: Yale University Press, 2006).

⁹⁹ Virgil, *The Aeneid*, trans. David Ferry (Chicago: University of Chicago Press, 2017).

Short note   ⁹⁹ Plato, *Republic* 3.212b–414b.
⁹⁹ Virgil, *Aeneid* 5.6–31.

Bibliography   ▶ Classical Greek and Latin works are not normally included in the bibliography except to reference the specific translation or commentary by a modern author.
Plato. *The Republic*. Translated by R. E. Allen. New Haven, CT: Yale University Press, 2006.
Virgil. *The Aeneid*. Translated by David Ferry. Chicago: University of Chicago Press, 2017.

Speech, academic talk, or course lecture

First note   ⁹⁹ Alison Dagnes, "Circles of Influence: How the Current Partisan Media System Divides Us" (paper presented at the annual meeting of the Northeastern Political Science Association, November 12, 2015).
⁹⁹ Gary Sick, lecture on US policy toward Iran (U.S. Foreign Policy Making in the Persian Gulf, course taught at Columbia University, New York, March 22, 2007).
▶ The title of Professor Sick's talk is not capitalized or in quotes because it is a regular course lecture and does not have a specific title. I have given a description, but you could simply call it a lecture and omit the description. For example: Gary Sick, untitled lecture (U.S. Foreign . . .).

Short note   ⁹⁹ Dagnes, "Circles of Influence"
▶ or, to differentiate it from Skorton's addresses in subsequent years:
⁹⁹ Skorton, "State of the University Speech," 2006.
⁹⁹ Sick, lecture on US policy toward Iran.

Bibliography   Dagnes, Alison. "Circles of Influence: How the Current Partisan Media System Divides Us." Paper presented at the annual meeting of the Northeastern Political Science Association, November 12, 2015.
Sick, Gary. Lecture on US policy toward Iran. U.S. Foreign Policy Making in the Persian Gulf, course taught at Columbia University, New York, March 22, 2007.

Personal communication or interview	First note	[99] Robert Alter, personal interview, October 21, 2015.

Personal communication or interview

First note

[99] Robert Alter, personal interview, October 21, 2015.
[99] Nicolas Sarkozy, telephone interview, May 5, 2013.
[99] George Lucas, video interview (Skype), October 27, 2016.
[99] Anonymous US soldier recently returned from Afghanistan, interview by author, February 19, 2017.
[99] Discussion with senior official at Department of Homeland Security, Washington, DC, January 7, 2010.

▶ Sometimes you may not wish to reveal the source of an interview or conversation, or you may have promised not to reveal your source. If so, then you should (a) reveal as much descriptive data as you can, such as "a police officer who works with an anti-gang unit," instead of just "a police officer," and (b) explain to readers in a footnote why you are omitting names, such as "All interviews with State Department officials were conducted with guarantees of anonymity because the officials were not authorized to disclose this information to the public."

[99] Ta-Nehisi Coates, "On Charlottesville, Trump, the Confederacy, Reparations & More," interview by Amy Goodman and Juan González, *Democracy Now!*, August 15, 2017, https://www.democracynow.org/2017/8/15/full_interview_ta_nehisi_coates_on.

Short note

[99] Robert Alter, personal interview, October 21, 2015.
[99] George Lucas, video interview, October 27, 2016.
[99] Nicolas Sarkozy, telephone interview, May 5, 2013.
[99] Anonymous US soldier, interview by author, February 19, 2017.
[99] Discussion with senior official at Department of Homeland Security, January 7, 2010.
[99] Coates, "On Charlottesville."

	Bibliography	► Interviews should be included in the bibliography if they are in print, online, or archived because they are available to other researchers. Personal interviews and communications that are not accessible to others should be described fully in the notes and omitted from the bibliography. Hence there is a bibliographic item for Coates but none for Alter, Sarkozy, Lucas, or the anonymous US soldier or senior official.

Coates, Ta-Nehisi. "On Charlottesville, Trump, the Confederacy, Reparations, & More." Interview by Amy Goodman and Juan González. *Democracy Now!*, August 15, 2017. https://www.democracynow.org/2017/8/15/full_interview_ta_nehisi_coates_on.

Poem	First note	[99] Elizabeth Bishop, "The Fish," in *The Complete Poems, 1927–1979* (New York: Noonday Press / Farrar, Straus and Giroux, 1983), 42–44. [99] Walt Whitman, "Song of Myself," in *Leaves of Grass* (Philadelphia: David McKay, 1891–92), sec. 51, p. 78, http://whitmanarchive.org/published/LG/1891/whole.html.
	Short note	[99] Bishop, "The Fish," 42–44. [99] Whitman, "Song of Myself," sec. 51, p. 78.
	Bibliography	Bishop, Elizabeth. "The Fish." In *The Complete Poems, 1927–1979*, 42–44. New York: Noonday Press / Farrar, Straus and Giroux, 1983. Walt Whitman. "Song of Myself." In *Leaves of Grass*, 29–79. Philadelphia: David McKay, 1891–92. http://whitmanarchive.org/published/LG/1891/whole.html.

Play, text	First note	[99] Shakespeare, *Hamlet, Prince of Denmark*, 2.1.1–9. ► Refers to act 2, scene 1, lines 1–9. ► Examples for citing a specific edition: [99] William Shakespeare, *Hamlet, Prince of Denmark*, ed. Constance Jordan (New York: Pearson/Longman, 2005).

Play, text (*continued*)

[99] William Shakespeare, *The Three-Text Hamlet: Parallel Texts of the First and Second Quartos and First Folio*, ed. Bernice W. Kliman and Paul Bertram (New York: AMS Press, 2003). [99] William Shakespeare, *Hamlet, Prince of Denmark* (1600–1601; University of Virginia Library, Electronic Text Center, 1998), http://etext.virginia.edu/toc/modeng/public/MobHaml.html.

Short note

[99] Shakespeare, *Hamlet*, 2.1.1–9.

Bibliography

Shakespeare, William. *Hamlet, Prince of Denmark*. Edited by Constance Jordan. New York: Pearson/Longman, 2005.

Shakespeare, William. *The Three-Text Hamlet: Parallel Texts of the First and Second Quartos and First Folio*. Edited by Bernice W. Kliman and Paul Bertram. New York: AMS Press, 2003.

Shakespeare, William. *Hamlet, Prince of Denmark*. 1600–1601. University of Virginia Library, Electronic Text Center, 1998. http://etext.virginia.edu/toc/modeng/public/MobHaml.html.

Performance of play or dance

First note

[99] *Romeo and Juliet*, choreography by Krzysztof Pastor, music by Sergei Prokofiev, Joffrey Ballet, Auditorium Theatre, Chicago, October 13, 2016. [99] *Fake*, written and directed by Eric Simonson, performed by Kate Arrington, Francis Guinan, and Alan Wilder, Steppenwolf Theatre, Chicago, October 28, 2009.

▶ If you are concentrating on one person or one position such as director, put that person's name first. For example, if you are concentrating on Kate Arrington's acting:

[99] Kate Arrington, performance, *Fake*, written and directed by Eric Simonson, . . .

Short note

[99] *Romeo and Juliet*.
[99] *Fake*.

Bibliography   *Romeo and Juliet*. Choreography by Krzysztof Pastor. Music by Sergei Prokofiev. Joffrey Ballet. Auditorium Theatre, Chicago, October 13, 2016.

Fake. Written and directed by Eric Simonson. Performed by Kate Arrington, Francis Guinan, and Alan Wilder. Steppenwolf Theatre, Chicago, October 28, 2009.

▸ or, if you are concentrating on Arrington's acting:

Kate Arrington, performance. *Fake*. Written and directed by Eric Simonson, . . .

▸ Live performances are often left out of the bibliography, since the performance cannot be consulted in person by the reader.

Television program

First note   [99] *Game of Thrones*, season 4, episode 10, "The Children," June 15, 2014.

▸ or a fuller citation:

[99] *Game of Thrones*, season 4, episode 10, "The Children," directed by Alex Graves, written by David Benioff and D. B. Weiss, featuring Peter Dinklage, Nikolaj Coster-Waldau, Lena Heady, Kit Harington, and Maisie Williams, aired June 15, 2014, on HBO.

[99] *30 Rock*, season 4, episode 1, "Season 4," directed by Don Scardino, written by Tina Fey, performed by Tina Fey, Tracy Morgan, Jane Krakowski, Jack McBrayer, Scott Adsit, Judah Friedlander, and Alec Baldwin, aired October 15, 2009 (NBC), http://www.hulu.com/30 -rock.

▸ Yes, this first episode of the fourth season was actually called "Season 4." Episode numbers are helpful. So are original air dates for shows you watched in a medium other than broadcast.

Short note   [99] *Game of Thrones*, "The Children."

[99] *30 Rock*, "Season 4."

Television program (*continued*)	Bibliography	*Game of Thrones*. Season 4, episode 10, "The Children," Directed by Alex Graves. Written by David Benioff and D. B. Weiss. Featuring Peter Dinklage, Nikolaj Coster-Waldau, Lena Heady, Kit Harington, and Maisie Williams. Aired June 15, 2014, on HBO. *30 Rock*. Season 4, episode 1, "Season 4." Directed by Don Scardino. Written by Tina Fey. Performed by Tina Fey, Tracy Morgan, Jane Krakowski, Jack McBrayer, Scott Adsit, Judah Friedlander, and Alec Baldwin. Aired October 15, 2009, on NBC. http://www.hulu.com/30-rock.
Film	First note	⁹⁹ *Godfather II*, directed by Francis Ford Coppola (1974; Los Angeles: Paramount Home Video, 2003), DVD. ⁹⁹ *Tig*, directed by Kristina Goolsby and Ashley York (Beachside Films, 2015), Netflix. ▸ If you wish to cite individual scenes, treat them like chapters in books. "Murder of Fredo," in *Godfather II* . . .
	Short note	⁹⁹ *Godfather II*. ⁹⁹ *Tig*.
	Bibliography	*Godfather II*, DVD. Directed by Francis Ford Coppola. Performed by Al Pacino, Robert De Niro, Robert Duvall, Diane Keaton. Screenplay by Francis Ford Coppola and Mario Puzo based on novel by Mario Puzo. 1974; Paramount Home Video, 2003. *Tig*. Netflix. Directed by Kristina Goolsby and Ashley York. Written by Jennifer Arnold. Performed by Tig Notaro, Stephanie Allynne, Zach Galifianakis, Sarah Silverman. Beachside Films, 2015. ▸ Title, director, studio, and year of release are all required. So is the year the video recording was released, if that's what you are citing.

▶ Optional: the actors, producers, screenwriters, editors, cinematographers, and other information. You can include what you need for your paper, in order of their importance to your analysis. Their names appear between the title and the distributor.

Artwork	First note	[99] Jacopo Robusti Tintoretto, *The Birth of John the Baptist*, ca. 1550, Hermitage, St. Petersburg.

▶ If the exact date of an artwork is not available, give an approximate one. A painting from "circa 1550" would be abbreviated "ca. 1550."

[99] Jacopo Robusti Tintoretto, *The Birth of John the Baptist*, 1550s, in Tom Nichols, *Tintoretto: Tradition and Identity* (London: Reaktion Books, 1999), 47.

▶ For a reproduction, cite where you found the work.

[99] Jacopo Robusti Tintoretto, *The Birth of John the Baptist* (detail), 1550s, Hermitage, St. Petersburg, http://cgfa.acropolisinc.com/t/p -tintore1.htm.

▶ Include a URL for art consulted online.

Short note   [99] Tintoretto, *Birth of John the Baptist*.

▶ Shorten note the same way for an original, reproduction, or artwork found online.

Bibliography   ▶ Do not include any artwork, sculptures, or photographs in the bibliography.

Photograph	First note	[99] Ansel Adams, *Monolith, the Face of Half Dome, Yosemite National Park*, 1927, Art Institute, Chicago.

[99] Ansel Adams, *Monolith, the Face of Half Dome, Yosemite National Park*, 1927, Art Institute, Chicago, http://www.hctc.commnet .edu/artmuseum/anseladams/details/pdf/ monlith.pdf.

Short note   [99] Adams, *Monolith*.

Bibliography   ▶ Artwork, sculptures, and photographs are not usually included in the bibliography.

Figures: map, chart, graph, or table	Credit for figure or table	▶ Citation for a map, chart, graph, or table normally appears as a credit below the item or within the text, but can be cited in a note if needed. *Source*: Ken Menkhaus, "Governance without Government in Somalia: Spoilers, State Building, and the Politics of Coping," *International Security* 31 (Winter 2006/7): 79, fig. 1. *Source*: "Presidential Election Results: Donald J. Trump Wins" (interactive map), *New York Times*, August 9, 2017, https://www.nytimes.com/elections/results/president. [99] Garrett Dash Nelson and Alasdair Rae, *An Economic Geography of the United States: From Commutes to Megaregions*, *Plos One*, accessed August 29, 2017, https://doi.org/10.1371/journal.pone.0166083.g001. [99] G. M. Wheeler, *Topographical Map of the Yosemite Valley and Vicinity*, preliminary edition, 1883, 43 × 55cm, 1:42,240 scale, David Rumsey Historical Map Collection, http://www.davidrumsey.com/luna/servlet/detail/RUMSEY~8~1~405~40014:Topographical-Map-Of-The-Yosemite-V. *Source*: Google Maps, map of 1427 E. 60th St., Chicago, IL 60637, accessed May 5, 2017, http://maps.google.com/. ▶ For maps, include cartographer (if known), the title or description of the map, the scale and size, and publication details or location. ▶ For undated maps consulted online, include an access or revision date.
	Short citation	▶ Use full citations for all figures.
	Bibliography	Menkhaus, Ken. "Governance without Government in Somalia: Spoilers, State Building, and the Politics of Coping." *International Security* 31 (Winter 2006/7): 74–106. ▶ Do not list any maps, charts, graphs or tables in the bibliography; *do* include any book, article, or other publication used as the source for such an item. Google Maps does not need to appear in the bibliography; the other sources do.

"Presidential Election Results: Donald J. Trump Wins." *New York Times*, August 9, 2017. https://www.nytimes.com/elections/results/president.

Musical recording

First note

⁹⁹ Robert Johnson, "Cross Road Blues," 1937, *Robert Johnson: King of the Delta Blues Singers*, Columbia Records 1654, 1961.

⁹⁹ Samuel Barber, "Cello Sonata, for cello and piano, op. 6," *Barber: Adagio for Strings, Violin Concerto, Orchestral and Chamber Works*, compact disc 2, St. Louis Symphony, cond. Leonard Slatkin, Alan Stepansky (cello), Israela Margalit (piano), EMI Classics 74287, 2001.

⁹⁹ Jimi Hendrix, "Purple Haze," 1969, *Woodstock: Three Days of Peace and Music*, compact disc 4 of 4, Atlantic/Wea, 1994.

⁹⁹ Vladimir Horowitz, Hungarian Rhapsody no. 2, by Franz Liszt, recorded live at Carnegie Hall, February 25, 1953, MP3 file (241 Kbps).

▸ Kbps stands for kilobits per second; MP3 is the name of the popular audio compression format. If the MP3 file is just a copy of a version from compact disc or LP, you can cite the original:

⁹⁹ Vladimir Horowitz, Hungarian Rhapsody no. 2, by Franz Liszt, recorded live at Carnegie Hall, February 25, 1953, compact disc, RCA Victor 60523-2-RG, 1991.

⁹⁹ Beyoncé, "Formation," TIDAL, track 11 on *Lemonade*, Parkwood Entertainment and Columbia Records, 2016.

▸ Include the service or file format for streaming audio.

Short note

⁹⁹ Johnson, "Cross Road Blues."
⁹⁹ Barber, "Cello Sonata, op. 6."
⁹⁹ Hendrix, "Purple Haze."
⁹⁹ Horowitz, Hungarian Rhapsody no. 2.
⁹⁹ Beyoncé, "Formation."

Bibliography

Johnson, Robert. "Cross Road Blues." 1937. *Robert Johnson: King of the Delta Blues Singers*. Columbia Records 1654, 1961.

Musical recording (*continued*)		Barber, Samuel. "Cello Sonata, for cello and piano, op. 6." *Barber: Adagio for Strings, Violin Concerto, Orchestral and Chamber Works*. Compact disc 2. St. Louis Symphony. Cond. Leonard Slatkin, Alan Stepansky (cello), Israela Margalit (piano). EMI Classics 74287, 2001. Hendrix, Jimi. "Purple Haze," 1969. *Woodstock: Three Days of Peace and Music*. Compact disc 4. Atlantic/Wea, 1994. Horowitz, Vladimir. Hungarian Rhapsody no. 2, by Franz Liszt. Recorded live at Carnegie Hall, February 25, 1953. MP3 file (241 Kbps). Beyoncé. "Formation." TIDAL. Track 11 on *Lemonade*. Parkwood Entertainment and Columbia Records, 2016.
Recording of reading, lecture, or audiobook	First note	[99] Franklin D. Roosevelt, "Fireside Chat: Outlining New Deal Program," May 7, 1933, Recorded Speeches and Utterances of Franklin D. Roosevelt, FDR Presidential Library and Museum, MP3 audio (23:00), http://www .fdrlibrary.marist.edu/archives/collections/ utterancesfdr.html. [99] George Eliot, *Middlemarch*, performed by Juliet Stevenson, Naxos Audiobooks, released on Audible.com, March 18, 2011. ▶ Cite recordings of readings, books, or lectures as you would musical recordings.
	Short note	[99] Roosevelt, "Fireside Chat." [99] Eliot, *Middlemarch*.
	Bibliography	Roosevelt, Franklin D. "Fireside Chat: Outlining New Deal Program." May 7, 1933. Recorded Speeches and Utterances of Franklin D. Roosevelt, FDR Presidential Library and Museum. MP3 audio (23:00). http://www.fdrlibrary.marist.edu/ archives/collections/utterancesfdr.html. Eliot, George. *Middlemarch*. Performed by Juliet Stevenson. Naxos Audiobooks. Released on Audible.com, March 18, 2011.

Music video, comments on music video	First note	[99] Arcade Fire, "Everything Now," music video, directed by the Sacred Egg, released June 1, 2017, https://youtu.be/zC3oBYR3CUk. [99] Rihanna, Kanye West, and Paul McCartney, "FourFiveSeconds," music video, directed by Inez & Vinoodh, produced by Stephanie Bargas and Jeff Lepine, February 3, 2015, http://vevo.ly/3aZlDK. [99] Bruno Mars, "That's What I Like," music video, directed by Bruno Mars and Jonathan Lia, March 1, 2017, https://youtu.be/PMivT7MJ41M. [99] Minimanaloto, March 3, 2017, comment on Mars, "That's What I Like."
	Short note	[99] Arcade Fire, "Everything Now." [99] Rihanna, Kanye West, and Paul McCartney, "FourFiveSeconds." [99] Mars, "That's What I Like." [99] Minimanaloto, comment on Mars, "That's What I Like."
	Bibliography	Arcade Fire. "Everything Now." Music video. Directed by the Sacred Egg, released June 1, 2017. https://youtu.be/zC3oBYR3CUk. Rihanna, Kanye West, and Paul McCartney. "FourFiveSeconds." Music video. Directed by Inez & Vinoodh. Produced by Stephanie Bargas and Jeff Lepine, released February 3, 2015, http://vevo.ly/3aZlDK. Mars, Bruno. "That's What I Like." Music video. Directed by Bruno Mars and Jonathan Lia, released March 1, 2017. https://youtu.be/PMivT7MJ41M. ▸ Viewers' comments on music videos are not included in bibliographies.
Sheet music	First note	[99] Johann Sebastian Bach, "Toccata and Fugue in D Minor," 1708, BWV 565, arranged by Ferruccio Benvenuto Busoni for solo piano (New York: G. Schirmer LB1629, 1942).
	Short note	[99] Bach, "Toccata and Fugue in D Minor."

Sheet music (*continued*)	Bibliography	Bach, Johann Sebastian. "Toccata and Fugue in D Minor." 1708. BWV 565. Arranged by Ferruccio Benvenuto Busoni for solo piano. New York: G. Schirmer LB1629, 1942. ▸ This piece was written in 1708 and has the standard Bach classification BWV 565. This particular arrangement was published by G. Schirmer in 1942 and has Schirmer's catalog number LB1629.
Liner notes	First note	[99] Steven Reich, liner notes for *Different Trains*, Elektra/Nonesuch 9 79176-2, 1988.
	Short note	[99] Reich, liner notes. ▸ or [99] Reich, liner notes, *Different Trains*.
	Bibliography	Reich, Steven. Liner notes for *Different Trains*. Elektra/Nonesuch 9 79176-2, 1988.
Advertisement	First note	[99] *Letters from Iwo Jima* advertisement, *New York Times*, February 6, 2007, B4. ▸ You may omit pagination from newspapers, if you wish, since these vary from edition to edition. [99] Vitamin Water, "Drink outside the Lines" advertisement, *Rolling Stone*, June 15, 2017, 17. [99] Tab cola, "Be a Mindsticker," television advertisement, ca. late 1960s, http://www.dailymotion.com/video/x2s3qi_1960s-tab-commercial-be-a-mindstick_ads.
	Short note	[99] *Letters from Iwo Jima* advertisement. [99] Vitamin Water, "Drink outside the Lines" advertisement. [99] Tab advertisement.
	Bibliography	▸ Advertisements are rarely included in bibliographies, but you may include them if they are especially important to your work. Letters from *Iwo Jima* advertisement. *New York Times*, February 6, 2007. Vitamin Water. "Drink outside the Lines" advertisement. *Rolling Stone*, June 15, 2017, 17.

Tab cola. "Be a Mindsticker." Television
advertisement, ca. late 1960s. http://www
.dailymotion.com/video/x2s3qi_1960s-tab
-commercial-be-a-mindstick_ads.

Government document	First note	[99] Senate Committee on Armed Services, *Hearings on S. 758, A Bill to Promote the National Security by Providing for a National Defense Establishment*, 80th Cong., 1st sess., 1947, S. Rep. 239, 13. ▸ "S. Rep. 239, 13" refers to report number 239, page 13. [99] *Financial Services and General Government Appropriations Act, 2008*, HR 2829, 110th Cong., 1st sess., *Congressional Record* 153 (June 28, 2007): H7347. [99] *American Health Care Act, 2017*, HR 1628, 115th Cong., 1st sess., June 8, 2017, Congress.Gov, https://www.congress.gov/bill/115th-congress/house-bill/1628/text. [99] Department of the Treasury, Office of Foreign Assets Control (OFAC), *Sanctions Actions Pursuant to Executive Order 13581, Federal Register* 82, no. 166 (August 29, 2017): 41019, https://www.gpo.gov/fdsys/pkg/FR-2017-08-29/pdf/2017-18289.pdf. [99] US Department of State, Daily Press Briefing, August 9, 2017, https://www.state.gov/r/pa/prs/dpb/2017/08/273288.htm.
	Short note	[99] Senate, *Hearings on S. 758*, 13. [99] *American Health Care Act*, HR 1628. [99] OFAC, *Sanctions Actions*. [99] US State Department, Daily Press Briefing, August 9, 2017.
	Bibliography	US Congress. Senate. Committee on Armed Services. *Hearings on S. 758, Bill to Promote the National Security by Providing for a National Defense Establishment*. 80th Cong., 1st sess., 1947. S. Rep. 239. US Congress. House. *Congressional Record*. 110th Cong., 1st sess. June 28, 2007. Vol. 153, no. 106. H7347.

Government document (*continued*)		*American Health Care Act, 2017*. HR 1628, 115th Cong., 1st sess. June 8, 2017. Congress.Gov, https://www.congress.gov/bill/115th-congress/house-bill/1628/text. Department of the Treasury, Office of Foreign Assets Control. *Sanctions Actions Pursuant to Executive Order 13581*. *Federal Register* 82, no. 166 (August 29, 2017): 41019. https://www.gpo.gov/fdsys/pkg/FR-2017-08-29/pdf/2017-18289.pdf. US Department of State. Daily press briefing. August 9, 2017. https://www.state.gov/r/pa/prs/dpb/2017/08/273288.htm.
Website, page or entire	First note	[99] "News and Advocacy," American Historical Association (website), accessed August 1, 2017, https://www.historians.org/news-and-advocacy. ▸ Many webpages do not have identifiable authors. List the organization that sponsors the website instead. ▸ Include the word *website* or *webpage* if it is not clear from the title. [99] Digital History (website), ed. Steven Mintz, accessed August 5, 2017, http://www.digitalhistory.uh.edu/. [99] Yale University, History Department home page, accessed August 5, 2017, http://www.yale.edu/history/. ▸ You may omit "home page" if it is obvious. [99] Charles Lipson, "News and Commentary: US and the World," accessed August 29, 2017, http:// www.charleslipson.com/News-links.htm. ▸ Include a publication date or date of revision or modification if possible. If none is available, include access date.
	Short note	[99] "News and Advocacy." [99] Digital History. [99] Yale History Department. [99] Lipson, "News and Commentary."

Bibliography
American Historical Association (website). "News and Advocacy." Accessed August 1, 2017. https://www.historians.org/news -and-advocacy

Digital History (website). Edited by Steven Mintz. Accessed August 5, 2017. http:// www.digitalhistory.uh.edu/.

Yale University. History Department home page. Accessed August 5, 2017. http:// www.yale.edu/history/.

Lipson, Charles. "News and Commentary: US and the World." Accessed August 29, 2017. http://www.charleslipson.com/News-links .htm.

▸ Website citations can be limited to the notes. If you choose to include a website in the bibliography, cite by the owner, author, or sponsor of the website.

Blog post or comment

First note
⁹⁹ Greg Weeks, "Venezuela's Core Support," *Two Weeks Notice: A Latin American Politics Blog*, August 2, 2017, http://weeksnotice .blogspot.com/2017/08/venezuelas-core -support.html.

▸ If this post had no title, it would be cited thus: Greg Weeks, untitled post, *Two Weeks Notice: A Latin American Politics blog* . . .

⁹⁹ Ana Arana, "The Deep Magic of Mexico," *The Big Roundtable* (blog), December 8, 2016, https://thebigroundtable.com/the-deep -magic-of-mexico-2bf1b341d1a1.

⁹⁹ Stefanie Fletcher, December 8, 2016 (11:30 a.m.), comment on Arana, "Deep Magic."

▸ Stefanie Fletcher made more than one comment on this post, so the time is included to specify which one.

▸ Comments are cited in reference to the original post.

Short note
⁹⁹ Weeks, "Venezuela's Core Support."
⁹⁹ Arana, "Deep Magic."
⁹⁹ Fletcher, comment on Arana, "Deep Magic."

Blog post or comment (*continued*)	Bibliography	▸ Blog posts are not usually part of the bibliography, but you may include them if the items are important in their own right or are especially significant for your paper. Here is the format: Weeks, Greg. "Venezuela's Core Support." *Two Weeks Notice: A Latin American Politics Blog*, August 2, 2017. http://weeksnotice.blogspot.com/2017/08/venezuelas-core-support.html. Arana, Ana. "The Deep Magic of Mexico." *The Big Roundtable* (blog), December 8, 2016. https://thebigroundtable.com/the-deep-magic-of-mexico-2bf1b341d1a1.
Video	First note	[99] *Duck and Cover*, Federal Civil Defense Administration/Archer Productions, 1951, video file, posted August 19, 2008, http://en.wikipedia.org/wiki/File: DuckandC1951.ogg. [99] Martin Shkreli on Three Counts of Security Fraud," NBC video news clip, August 4, 2017, http://www.nbcnews.com/video/jury-convicts-martin-shkreli-on-three-counts-of-securities-fraud-1017719875664. [99] Franchesca Ramsey, "Turn Your Phone!" Franchesca Ramsey video blog, accessed August 5, 2017, 3:07, http://www.franchesca.net/videos-photos/. [99] Tricia Wang, "The Human Insights Missing from Big Data," filmed September, 2016, TEDxCambridge, TED video, 16:12, https://www.ted.com/talks/tricia_wang_the_human_insights_missing_from_big_data.
	Short note	[99] *Duck and Cover*. [99] "Jury Convicts Martin Shkreli," August 4, 2017." [99] Ramsey, "Turn Your Phone!" [99] Wang, "Human Insights."
	Bibliography	*Duck and Cover*. Federal Civil Defense Administration / Archer Productions, 1951. Video file. Posted August 19, 2008. http://en.wikipedia.org/wiki/File:DuckandC1951.ogg.

"Jury Convicts Martin Shkreli on Three Counts of Security Fraud." NBC video news clip, August 4, 2017. http://www.nbcnews .com/video/jury-convicts-martin-shkreli -on-three-counts-of-securities-fraud -1017719875664.

Ramsey, Franchesca. "Turn Your Phone!" Franchesca Ramsey video blog. Accessed August 5, 2017. 3:07. http://www .franchesca.net/videos-photos/.

Wang, Tricia. "The Human Insights Missing from Big Data." Filmed September, 2016, at TEDxCambridge. TED video, 16:12. https://www.ted.com/talks/tricia_wang _the_human_insights_missing_from_big _data.

Multimedia app (video game, other stand-alone application)	First note	[99] *Madden NFL 18* (EA Sports, November 2017), PlayStation 4, Xbox One. [99] *Geocaching*, v. 5.6.1 (Seattle: Groundspeak, 2017), Android, iOS 9.0 or later. ▸ Include any relevant information such as version number, release date, and information about the device or operating system necessary to run the app.
	Short note	[99] *Madden NFL 18.* [99] *Geocaching.*
	Bibliography	EA Sports. *Madden NFL 18.* November 2017, PlayStation 4, Xbox One. Groundspeak. *Geocaching*, v. 5.6.1. Seattle: Groundspeak, 2017. Android, iOS 9.0 or later.
Podcast	First note	[99] Brian Reed, host, "Has Anybody Called You?" *S-Town*, podcast, produced by Brian Reed and Julie Snyder, Serial Productions, March 28, 2017, https://stownpodcast.org /chapter/2. [99] Ellen DeGeneres, "Ellen's Parenting Advice," *The Ellen Show Podcast*, Telepictures Productions, video podcast, June 26, 2015, iTunes. ▸ If no date can be found for the podcast, include the date accessed.

Podcast *(continued)*	Short note	[99] Reed, "Chapter 2."
		[99] DeGeneres, "Ellen's Parenting Advice."
	Bibliography	Reed, Brian, host. "Has Anybody Called You?" *S-Town*, podcast. Brian Reed and Julie Snyder, Serial Productions. March 28, 2017. https://stownpodcast.org/chapter/2.
		DeGeneres, Ellen. "Ellen's Parenting Advice." *The Ellen Show Podcast*. Telepictures Productions. Video podcast. June 26, 2015. iTunes.

Social media (Facebook, Instagram, Twitter)	First note	[99] Neil deGrasse Tyson (@neiltyson), "Always seemed to me that millipedes have more legs than are necessary," Twitter, July 7, 2017, 1:25 p.m., twitter.com/neiltyson/status/883421859072458752.
		[99] Smithsonian National Museum of African American History and Culture, "For African Americans, the pleasure of swimming at a public pool or beach was not always a right," Facebook, July 28, 2017, 1:50 p.m., https://www.facebook.com/NMAAHC/.
		[99] Bruce Jackson, "Kennywood closed and paved over the pool rather than integrate," July 30, 2017, 11:49 a.m., comment on Smithsonian, "For African Americans."
		[99] Cory Richards (@coryrichards), "A quiet if not solemn day on Everest," Instagram photo, May 24, 2017, https://www.instagram.com/p/BUekBZLgDOW/?hl=en.
		▸ Publicly available social media content, including comments on others' posts, should be cited in this way. Private content such as direct messages should be cited as a form of personal communication.
		▸ Comments are cited in reference to the original post.
		▸ If there is no title, use the text of the post, up to 160 characters.
		▸ If no real name is known, use the screen name only.
	Short note	[99] Tyson, "Always seemed to me."
		[99] Smithsonian, "For African Americans."
		[99] Jackson, comment on Smithsonian, "For African Americans."
		[99] Richards, "A quiet if not solemn day."

	Bibliography	▶ Do not include individual comments posted to social networking sites in the bibliography. It is fine, however, to include a particular person's page.
		Richards, Corey. Instagram page. https://www.instagram.com/coryrichards/?hl=en.

Email, texts (direct messages)	First note	[99] Jim Abrams, "Fw: a Favor," email from Jim Abrams to Mayor Rahm Emanuel, April 28, 2015, https://assets.documentcloud.org/documents/3516674/Abrams-amp-Bank-Phoenix-Electric.pdf.
		▶ No access date is required when citing email messages.
		▶ Include the URL if the email has been archived.
		[99] Kathy Leis, email message to author, May 5, 2017.
		[99] Kathy Leis, text message to author, May 5, 2017.
		[99] Alison Viup, Facebook direct message to author, July 20, 2016.
		▶ You may include the time of an electronic message if it is important or differentiates it from others. For example:
		[99] Michael Lipson, text message to Jonathan Lipson, May 5, 2017, 11:23 a.m.
		▶ Save copies of electronic messages that you intend to cite.
	Short note	[99] Jim Abrams to Rahm Emanuel, April 28, 2015.
		[99] Kathy Leis, email message to author, May 3, 2017.
		▶ You may be able to shorten these notes. If you are citing only one person named Leis, for instance, then you can drop the first name. But if you are citing messages from Alan Leis, Kathy Leis, Elizabeth Leis, and Julia Leis, then it is much clearer to include their first names, even in short notes.
		[99] Michael Lipson, instant message to Jonathan Lipson, May 5, 2017.
		[99] Michael Lipson, text message to Jonathan Lipson, May 5, 2017, 11:23 a.m.

Email, texts (direct messages) (*continued*)	Bibliography	► Personal emails, text and other instant messages, and emails to mailing lists are not included in the bibliography unless they can be retrieved by third parties. Abrams, Jim. "Fw: a Favor." Email from Jim Abrams to Mayor Rahm Emanuel, April 28, 2015. https://assets.documentcloud.org/ documents/3516674/Abrams-amp-Bank -Phoenix-Electric.pdf.
Electronic forum or mailing list	First note	[99] Quinn Ngo, answer to "What Are Some Unknown Truths about College Life?," Quora, July 14, 2017, https://www.quora.com/What -are-some-unknown-truths-about-college-life. [99] Mablegrable, "Cozy spot for a morning coffee," Reddit photo, August 4, 2017, https:// i.redd.it/okqb36mkbndz.jpg. [99] VeganSweets, "There's nothing like nature and some coffee/tea," August 4, 2017, 1:28 p.m., comment on Mablegrable, "Cozy Spot." [99] Mark Aaron Polger, "CALL: Call for Proposals," American Library Association mailing list archives, ACRL Campaign for Libraries list, May 10, 2017, http://lists.ala.org/sympa/arc/ academicpr/2017-05/msg00005.html. ► Posts on private email lists or forums are cited as personal communication just as an email or text message would.
	Short note	[99] Ngo, Quora, July 14, 2017. [99] VeganSweets, comment on Mablegrable, "Cozy Spot." [99] Polger, ALA mailing list, May 10, 2017.
	Bibliography	► Do not include individual comments posted to forums or mailing lists in the bibliography. You may include an entire thread or forum if it is cited extensively. Quora. "What Are Some Unknown Truths about College Life?" July 14, 2017. https:// www.quora.com/What-are-some-unknown -truths-about-college-life.

CHICAGO: CITATIONS OF TABLES AND NOTES

Citation	Refers to
106	page 106
106n	only note appearing on page 106
107n32	note number 32 on page 107, a page with several notes
89, table 6.2	table 6.2, which appears on page 89; similar for graphs and figures

CHICAGO: COMMON ABBREVIATIONS IN CITATIONS

and others	et al.	edited by	ed.	notes	nn.	part	pt.
appendix	app.	edition	ed.	number	no.	pseudonym	pseud.
book	bk.	editor(s)	ed(s).	opus	op.	translator	trans.
chapter	chap.	especially	esp.	opuses	opp.	versus	vs.
compare	cf.	figure	fig.	page	p.	volume	vol.
document	doc.	note	n.	pages	pp.		

Note: All abbreviations are lowercase, followed by a period. Most form their plurals by adding z-s. The exceptions are note (n. → nn.), opus (op. → opp.), page (p. → pp.), and translator (same abbreviation). (Another exception: when the abbreviation *n.* or *nn.* follows a page number with no intervening space, the period is dropped.)

In citing poetry, do not use abbreviations for "line" or "lines" since a lowercase *l* is easily confused with the number 1.

FAQS ABOUT CHICAGO-STYLE CITATIONS

Are there any differences between the rules for citations in *The Chicago Manual of Style* and those in Kate L. Turabian's *Manual for Writers of Research Papers, Theses, and Dissertations*?

No. Although there used to be some minor differences between them (for example, on whether or not to include access dates for online sources), Turabian and Chicago citation styles are now essentially the same.

For an online source, do I need to list the date when I accessed the source?

Generally not. One exception is when you can't find an official date on the source stating when it was published, posted, or most recently modified. Then the access date is necessary to help establish at least some timeframe for when the material on the site was viewable. Also, instructors sometimes require listing access dates even when those other kinds of dates are available, so it's a good idea to ask.

Why do you put the state after some publishers and not after others?

The Chicago Manual of Style recommends using state names for all but the largest, best-known cities. To avoid confusion, it uses Cambridge, MA, for

Harvard and MIT University Presses but just Cambridge for Cambridge University Press in the ancient English university town. Also, you can drop the state name if it is already included in the publisher's title, such as Ann Arbor: University of Michigan Press.

What if a book is forthcoming?
Use "forthcoming" just as you would use the year. Here's a bibliographic entry:

> Godot, Shlomo. *Still Waiting.* London: Verso, forthcoming.

What if the date or place of publication is missing?
Same idea as "forthcoming." Where you would normally put the place or date, use "n.p." (no place) or "n.d." (no date). For example: (Montreal, QC: McGill-Queen's University Press, n.d.).

One book I cite has a title that ends with a question mark. Do I still put a period or a comma after it?
Comma, yes; period, no.

Are notes single-spaced or double-spaced? What about the bibliography?
Space your footnotes and endnotes the same way you do your text.

As for your bibliography, I think it is easiest to read if you single-space within entries and put a double space between the entries. But check what your department or publisher requires. It may require double-spacing for everything.

I'm reading Mark Twain. Do I cite Twain or Samuel Clemens?
When pseudonyms are well known such as Mark Twain or Mother Teresa, you can use them alone, without explanation, if you wish.

If you want to include both the pseudonym and the given name, the rule is simple. Put the better-known name first, followed by the lesser-known one in brackets. It doesn't matter if the "real" name is the lesser-known one.

> George Eliot [Mary Ann Evans]
> Isak Dinesen [Karen Christence Dinesen, Baroness Blixen-Finecke]
> Le Corbusier [Charles-Edouard Jeanneret]
> Benjamin Disraeli [Lord Beaconsfield]
> Lord Palmerston [Henry John Temple]
> Krusty the Clown [Herschel S. Krustofski]

If you wish to include the pseudonym in a bibliographic entry, it reads:

> Aleichem, Sholom [Solomon Rabinovitz]. *Fiddler on the Roof . . .*

4 MLA CITATIONS FOR THE HUMANITIES

The Modern Language Association (MLA) has developed a citation style that is widely used in the humanities. Instead of footnotes or endnotes, it uses in-text citations such as (Strier 125). Full information about each item appears in the bibliography, which MLA calls "Works Cited." Like other bibliographies, it contains three essential nuggets of information about each item: the author, title, and publication data. To illustrate, let's use a book by Amitav Ghosh. The full entry in the Works Cited is

> Ghosh, Amitav. *The Great Derangement: Climate Change and the Unthinkable.* U of Chicago P, 2016.

The eighth edition of the *MLA Handbook*, published in 2016, introduced an overarching approach to citing any source, no matter its format. This represented a major change, since MLA style used to require that you include the medium of publication—print, web, email, television, etc.— along with the full facts of publication. Because content now comes in so many forms, and moves between formats so easily, MLA now works from the idea that writers need an all-encompassing and flexible method for developing citations rather than a list of rigid rules.

In-text citations are brief and simple. Just insert (Ghosh) at the end of the sentence to cite the entire book, or (Ghosh 12) to refer to page 12. If your paper happens to cite several books by Ghosh, be sure your reader knows which one you are referring to. If that's not clear in the sentence, then include a very brief title: (Ghosh, *Great Derangement* 12).

MLA citations can be even briefer—and they should be, whenever possible. They can omit the author and the title as long as it's clear which work is being cited. For example:

> As Ghosh notes, climate change is rarely a topic in fiction classified as "literary" (7–9).

You can omit the in-text reference entirely if the author and title are clear and you are not citing specific pages. For instance:

Gibbon's *Decline and Fall of the Roman Empire* established new standards of documentary evidence for historians.

In this case there's nothing to put in an in-text reference that isn't already in the sentence. So, given MLA's consistent emphasis on brevity, you simply skip the reference. You still include Gibbon in your Works Cited.

Because in-text references are so brief, you can string several together in one parenthesis: (Bevington 17; Bloom 75; Vendler 51). The references are separated by semicolons.

If Ghosh's book were a three-volume work, then the citation to volume 3, page 17, would be (Ghosh 3: 17). If you need to differentiate this work from others by the same author, then include the title: (Ghosh, *Great Derangement* 3: 17). If you wanted to cite the volume but not a specific page, then use (Ghosh, vol. 3) or (Ghosh, *Great Derangement*, vol. 3). Why include "vol." here? So readers won't think you are citing page 3 of a one-volume work.

If several authors have the same last name, simply add their first initial to differentiate them: (C. Brontë, *Jane Eyre*), (E. Brontë, *Wuthering Heights*). Of course, full information about the authors and their works appears at the end, in the Works Cited.

Books like *Jane Eyre* appear in countless editions, and your readers may wish to look up passages in theirs. To make that easier, the MLA recommends that you add some information after the normal page citation. You might say, for example, that the passage appears in chapter 1.

Let's say that you quoted a passage from the first chapter of *Jane Eyre*, which appeared on page 7 in the edition you are using. Insert a semicolon after the page and add the chapter number, using a lowercase abbreviation for chapter: (E. Brontë, *Wuthering Heights* 7; ch. 1).

For Shakespeare, you can skip page numbers and cite by act, scene, and lines, separated by periods (*Romeo and Juliet* 1.3.12–15). A similar pattern can be used for other works of poetry or verse that include numbered lines and other divisions. To cite lines alone, spell out "line" or "lines" (lines 12–15).

When you refer to online documents, there are often no pages to cite. As a substitute, include a section or paragraph number, if there is one. Just put a comma after the author's name, then list the section or paragraph: (Padgett, sec. 9.7) or (Snidal, pars. 12–18). If the online document is a PDF file, go ahead and list the page numbers since those will be the same for all users: (Wang 14). If there's no numbering system, though, just list the author.

In-text citations normally appear at the end of sentences and are followed by the punctuation for the sentence itself. To illustrate:

A full discussion of these issues appears in *Miss Thistlebottom's Hobgoblins* (Bernstein).

In this style you can still use regular footnotes or endnotes for limited purposes. They can be used *only* for commentary, not for citations. If you need to cite some materials within the note itself, use in-text citations there just as you would in the text.

For brevity—a paramount virtue of the MLA system—the names of publishers are also compressed: Princeton University Press becomes Princeton UP, the University of Chicago Press becomes U of Chicago P. For the same reason, most month names are abbreviated.

MLA's penchant for brevity extends to referencing electronic information—to a point. URLs or DOIs are necessary for online sources, but MLA does not include "http://" or "https://" in URLs (though see the exception for DOIs). Access dates are now optional, although encouraged when no date of publication, posting, or modification can be found.

I have provided detailed information and examples in a table below. Because MLA style is often used in the humanities, where citations to plays, poems, paintings, and films are common, I include all of those genres. If you want still more examples or less common items, consult the handbook.

To make it easy to find the citations you need, I've listed them here alphabetically, along with the pages where they are described. At the end of the chapter I have listed some common MLA abbreviations.

INDEX OF MLA CITATIONS IN THIS CHAPTER

MLA: WORKS CITED AND IN-TEXT CITATIONS

| Book, one author | Works Cited | Lipson, Charles. *How to Write a BA Thesis: A Practical Guide from Your First Ideas to Your Finished Paper.* U of Chicago P, 2005.
Collins, Christopher. *Neopoetics: The Evolution of the Literate Imagination.* Columbia UP, 2016.
Fitzpatrick, Meghan. *Invisible Scars: Mental Trauma and the Korean War.* U of British Columbia P, 2017.
▸ MLA style omits the publisher's location, unless the book was published before 1900, in which case the city may be listed in place of the publisher's name:
Barcelona, 1870 |
| | In-text | (Lipson 80–82) or (80–82)
▸ Refers to pages 80–82.
▸ If it is necessary to differentiate this book from others by the same author, then cite thus:
(Lipson, *How* 22–23) |

▸ To shorten a title in MLA, include the first
noun with any preceding adjectives. If the title
does not begin with a noun phrase, just use
the first word, as long as it's clear which work
you're referencing.
(Collins 26) or (26)
(Fitzpatrick 136) or (136)

Books, several by same author	Works Cited	Talbot, Ian. *A History of Modern South Asia: Politics, States, Diasporas.* Yale UP, 2016. ---, editor. *The Independence of India and Pakistan: New Approaches and Reflections.* Oxford UP, 2013. ---. *Pakistan: A Modern History.* Palgrave Macmillan, 2010. ▸ The repetition of the author's name uses three hyphens, followed by a period. If the repeated name is that of an editor or translator, place a comma after the three hyphens instead of a period.
	In-text	(Talbot, *History* 34; Talbot, *Independence* 3–5; Talbot, *Pakistan* 456)

Book, multiple authors	Works Cited	Young, Harvey, and Queen Meccasia Zabriskie. *Black Theater Is Black Life: An Oral History of Chicago Theater and Dance, 1970–2010.* Northwestern UP, 2013. Fischer, John Martin, and Benjamin Mitchell-Yellin. *Near-Death Experiences: Understanding Visions of the Afterlife.* Oxford UP, 2016. Hall, Jacqueline Dowd, et al. *Like a Family: The Making of a Southern Cotton Mill World.* U of North Carolina P, 1987. ▸ When there are three or more authors, as there are for *Like a Family*, use "et al." after naming the first one.
	In-text	(Young and Zabriskie, *Black Theater* 15–26) or (Young and Zabriskie 15–26) (Fischer and Mitchell-Yellin 15–18) (Hall et al. 67)

Book, multiple editions	Works Cited	Strunk, William, Jr., and E. B. White. *The Elements of Style*. 50th anniversary ed., Longman, 2009.
		Saller, Carol Fisher. *The Subversive Copy Editor: Advice from Chicago*. 2nd ed., U of Chicago P, 2016.
		Head, Dominic, editor. *The Cambridge Guide to Literature in English*. 3rd ed., Cambridge UP, 2006.
		▶ If this were a multivolume work, then the volume number would come after the edition: 3rd ed., vol. 2.
	In-text	(Strunk and White 12)
		(Saller 97)
		(Head 15)
Book, edited	Works Cited	Ross, Jeffrey Ian, editor. *Routledge Handbook of Graffiti and Street Art*. Routledge, 2016.
		Gilbert, Sandra, and Susan Gubar, editors. *Feminist Literary Theory and Criticism: A Norton Reader*. Norton, 2007.
		Cheng, Jim, et al., editors. *An Annotated Bibliography for Taiwan Film Studies*. Columbia UP, 2016.
		▶ If there are three or more editors, name the first editor followed by "et al."
	In-text	(Ross 93)
		(Gilbert and Gubar 72)
		(Cheng et al. 12)
Book, anonymous or no author	Works Cited	*Through Our Enemies' Eyes: Osama Bin Laden, Radical Islam, and the Future of America*. Brassey's, 2003.
		The Secret Lives of Teachers. U of Chicago P, 2015.
		▶ Do not use "anonymous" as the author. If the author is unknown, alphabetize by title but ignore any initial article (*A*, *An*, or *The*). So *The Holy Koran* is alphabetized under "H."
	In-text	(*Through Our Enemies' Eyes*)
		(*Secret Lives*)

E-book	Works Cited	Miranda, Lin-Manuel, and Jeremy McCarter. *Hamilton: The Revolution*. Kindle ed., Grand Central Publishing, 2016. Auspitz, Kate. *Wallis's War: A Novel of Diplomacy and Intrigue*. iBooks ed., U of Chicago P, 2015. ▸ MLA treats an e-book as an edition (abbreviated *ed.*).
	In-text	(Miranda and McCarter) (Auspitz, ch. 3) ▸ If the version you are using lacks page numbers or uses reflowable text, cite a chapter or other indicator instead.
Book, online	Works Cited	James, Henry. *The Turn of the Screw*. Martin Secker, 1915. *Internet Archive*, archive.org/details/in.ernet.dli.2015.95031. Skrentny, John David. *After Civil Rights: Racial Realism in the New American Workplace*. Princeton UP, 2014. *eBook Academic Collection, EBSCOhost*. ▸ Following the publication details for the book, list the website that hosts it, followed by the URL. ▸ If you consulted the book through a library database, you don't need to list a URL, especially if the URL for the specific item is very long.
	In-text	(James 10) (Skrentny 105)
Multivolume work	Works Cited	Cunningham, Noble E., Jr., editor. *Circular Letters of Congressmen to Their Constituents, 1789–1829*. Omohundro Institute of Early American History and Culture / U of North Carolina P, 2013. 3 vols. ▸ If there is more than one publisher, include both with a slash between them.
	In-text	(Cunningham) or (Cunningham 3: 21) ▸ This refers to volume 3, page 21. (Cunningham, vol. 3)

Multivolume work (*continued*)		▸ When a volume is referenced without a specific page, then use "vol." so the volume won't be confused for a page number.
Single volume in a multivolume work	Works Cited	Caro, Robert A. *The Passage of Power*. 2012. *The Years of Lyndon Johnson*, vol. 4, Knopf, 1982–. 5 vols. projected. Iriye, Akira. *The Globalizing of America*. 1993. *Cambridge History of American Foreign Relations*, edited by Warren I. Cohen, vol. 3, Cambridge UP, 1993. 4 vols. ▸ Because these volumes have their own titles, MLA does not require the information for the other volumes. If you want, just cite the single title, with no volume number: Caro, Robert A. *The Passage of Power*. Knopf, 2012. Iriye, Akira. *The Globalizing of America*. Cambridge UP, 1993.
	In-text	(Caro) (Iriye)
Reprint of earlier edition	Works Cited	Barzun, Jacques. *Simple and Direct: A Rhetoric for Writers*. 1985. U of Chicago P, 1994. Smith, Adam. *An Inquiry into the Nature and Causes of the Wealth of Nations*. 1776. Edited by Edwin Cannan, U of Chicago P, 1976.
	In-text	(Barzun, *Simple*) or (Barzun) (Smith, *Inquiry*) or (Smith)
Translated volume	Works Cited	Gan, Aleksei. *Constructivism*. 1922. Translated by Christina Lodder, Editorial Tenov, 2014. Tocqueville, Alexis de. *Democracy in America*. Edited by J. P. Mayer, translated by George Lawrence, Harper, 2000. ▸ Editor and translator are listed in the order in which they appear on the book's title page. *Beowulf: A New Verse Translation*. Translated by Seamus Heaney, Farrar, 2000.

▶ *Beowulf* is an anonymous poem. The translator's name normally comes after the title. But
there is an exception. If you wish to comment
on the translator's work, then place the translator's name first. For example:
Heaney, Seamus, translator. *Beowulf: A New
Verse Translation*. Farrar, 2000.
Lodder, Christina, translator. *Constructivism*.
By Aleksei Gan, 1922. Editorial Tenov, 2014.

In-text
(Gan, *Constructivism*) or (Gan)
(Tocqueville, *Democracy in America*) or
(Tocqueville)
(Heaney, *Beowulf*) or (*Beowulf*)
(Lodder)

Chapter in
edited book
Works Cited
Jones, Kima. "Homegoing, AD." *The Fire This
Time: A New Generation Speaks about
Race*, edited by Jesmyn Ward, Scribner,
2016, pp. 15–18.

In-text
(Jones, 16)

Journal article
Works Cited
Sampsell, Gary. "Popular Music in the Time of
J. S. Bach: The Leipzig Mandora Manuscript." *Bach*, vol. 48, no. 1, 2017, pp. 1–35.
Domínguez Torres, Mónica. "Havana's For-
tunes: 'Entangled Histories' in Copley's
Watson and the Shark." *American Art*, vol.
30, no. 2, Summer 2016, pp. 8–13.
▶ If the article title includes a term in quotation
marks, use single quotation marks in your
citation.
Ünal, Yusuf. "Sayyid Quṭb in Iran: Translating
the Islamic Ideologue in the Islamic Republic." *Journal of Islamic and Muslim Studies*,
vol. 1, no. 2, Nov. 2016, pp. 35–60, https://
doi.org/10.2979/jims.1.2.04.
Judd, David, and James Rocha. "Autonomous
Pigs." *Ethics and the Environment*, vol. 22,
no. 1, Spring 2017, pp. 1–18, https://doi.org/
10.2979/ethicsenviro.22.1.01.

Journal article *(continued)*		► A DOI is preferable to another kind of URL if one is listed. Add https://doi.org/ to the DOI, despite the normal MLA rule of dropping https:// from URLs.

► A DOI is preferable to another kind of URL if one is listed. Add https://doi.org/ to the DOI, despite the normal MLA rule of dropping https:// from URLs.

► If there are three or more authors, list as "Judd, David, et al."

Tyler, Tom. "Snakes, Skins and the Sphinx: Nietzsche's Ecdysis." *Journal of Visual Culture*, vol. 5, no. 3, Dec. 2006, pp. 365–85. Abstract.

► To cite an abstract, include the word *Abstract* after the article information.

In-text

(Sampsell) or (Sampsell 31)

(Domínguez Torres 12)

(Ünal) or (Ünal 58) or (Ünal, "Sayyid Quṭb" 58)

► The title may be needed to differentiate this article from others by the same author.

(Judd and Rocha, 3–5)

(Tyler)

Journal article, foreign language

Works Cited

Joosten, Jan. "Le milieu producteur du Penta-teuque grec." *Revue des Études Juives*, vol. 165, nos. 3–4, juillet–décembre 2006, pp. 349–61.

► For inclusive page numbers, MLA requires the full second number up to 99, but only the last two digits for larger numbers, as long as the range is clear.

In-text

(Joosten) or (Joosten 356)

Newspaper or magazine article

Works Cited

"Retired U.S. General Is Focus of Inquiry over Iran Leak." *The New York Times*, 28 June 2013, p. A18.

► If an article has no author, list it by title.

Halbfinger, David M. "Politicians Are Doing Hollywood Star Turns." *The New York Times*, 6 Feb. 2007, natl. ed., pp. B1+.

► Use European-style dates: day month year.

► The plus sign indicates that the article continues, but not on the next page (this one continues on B7). If the article continued on B2 and ran to B3, you'd write B1–B3.

Halper, Evan. "Congress Takes Aim at the Clean Air Act, Putting the Limits of California's Power to the Test." *Los Angeles Times*, 3 Aug. 2017, 3:00 a.m. PDT, www.latimes .com/politics/la-na-pol-smog-republicans -20170803-story.html.

   ► Include a time stamp for articles that may be updated frequently.

   ► You do not need to include page numbers for articles consulted online.

In-text	("Retired U.S. General" A18)
	(Halbfinger B7) or (Halbfinger, "Politicians" B7) if you cite more than one article by this author.
	(Halper)

Review	Works Cited	Pugh, Allison J. Review of *The Gender Trap: Parents and the Pitfalls of Raising Boys and Girls*, by Emily W. Kane. *American Journal of Sociology*, vol. 119, no. 6, May 2014, pp. 1773–75.
		Paxton, Robert O. Review of *The Nazi-Fascist New Order for European Culture*, by Benjamin G. Martin. *New York Review of Books*, 26 Oct. 2017, www.nybooks.com/articles/ 2017/10/26/nazi-fascist-cultural-axis.
	In-text	(Pugh 1774) or (Pugh, "Gender Trap" 1774)
		(Paxton) or (Paxton, "Nazi-Fascist New Order")

Unpublished paper, thesis, or dissertation	Works Cited	Levine, Daniel H. "What Pope Francis Brings to Latin America." CLALS Working Paper Series 11, 12 Apr. 2016, papers.ssrn.com/sol3/ papers.cfm?abstract_id=2761467.
		Sierra, Luis Manuel. *Indigenous Neighborhood Residents in the Urbanization of La Paz, Bolivia, 1910–1950*. 2013. State U of New York at Binghamton, PhD dissertation, *ProQuest*, search.proquest.com/docview/ 1507870239?accountid=14657.
	In-text	(Levine)
		(Sierra) or (Sierra 49)

Archival materials and manuscript collections	Works Cited	Franklin, Isaac. Letter to R. C. Ballard. 28 Feb. 1831, Rice Ballard Papers. Southern Historical Collection, Wilson Lib. U of North Carolina, Chapel Hill. MS. Series 1.1, folder 1. Lamson, Mary Swift. "An Account of the Beginning of the B.Y.W.C.A." 1891, Manuscript. Boston YWCA Papers. Schlesinger Lib, Radcliffe Institute for Advanced Study, Harvard U. Cambridge, MA. Szold, Henrietta. Letter to Rose Jacobs. 3 Feb. 1932. Rose Jacobs–Alice L. Seligsberg Collection. Judaica Microforms. Brandeis Lib. Waltham, MA. Microform, reel 1, book 1. Szold, Henrietta. Letter to Rose Jacobs. 9 Mar. 1936. Central Zionist Archives, Jerusalem. A/125/112. Copland, Aaron. "At the Thought of Mozart." Manuscript / mixed material, Library of Congress, Washington, DC, www.loc.gov/item/copland.writo036. Accessed 13 Oct. 2017.
	In-text	(Franklin) or (Franklin to Ballard) or (Franklin to Ballard, 28 Feb. 1831) (Lamson) or (Lamson 2) (Szold) or (Szold to Jacobs) or (Szold to Jacobs, 3 Feb. 1932) (Szold) or (Szold to Jacobs) or (Szold to Jacobs, 9 Mar. 1936) (Taraval) or (Taraval, par. 23) ▸ This manuscript uses paragraph numbers, not pages. (Taft) or (Taft 149)
Encyclopedia and dictionary	Works Cited	*Encyclopaedia Britannica*, 15th ed., 1987. *Merriam-Webster*, www.merriamwebster.com. *Oxford English Dictionary*, 2nd ed., 1989. ▸ Cite the work as a whole in the list of works cited; the entries themselves are mentioned or described in the text. ▸ Edition and year are required for print resources. ▸ You can omit the publisher for well-known encyclopedias, dictionaries, and other references.

▶ If you do want to include the specific entry in your works cited, you can do it like this:

"App." *Merriam-Webster.* www.merriam-webster .com/dictionary/app. Accessed 24 Oct. 2017.

▶ For undated entries consulted online, include an access date.

"pluck, n.1." *OED Online,* www.oed.com/view/ Entry/145996. Accessed 24 Oct. 2017.

▶ There are two separate entries for the noun "pluck," and I am citing the first, hence "n.1." The second is for an obscure fish.

Kania, Andrea. "The Philosophy of Music." Revised 11 June 2017. *Stanford Encyclopedia of Philosophy,* plato.stanford.edu/entries/ music.

In-text	("App") or (*Merriam-Webster*)
	("Pluck") or (*Oxford English Dictionary*)
	(Kania)

Bible, Koran (Qur'an)

Works Cited

Tanakh: The Holy Scriptures: The New JPS Translation according to the Traditional Hebrew Text. Jewish Publication Society, 1985.

▶ The Bible, Koran, and other sacred texts do *not* usually appear in Works Cited unless you need to cite a particular version or translation.

In-text

(*Tanakh,* Genesis 1.1, 1.3–5, 2.4), then Genesis 1.1, 1.3–5, 2.4.

▶ Books may be abbreviated, such as Gen. 1.1, 1.3–5, 2.4.

▶ Abbreviations for the next four books are Ex., Lev., Num., and Deut. Abbreviations for other books are easily found with a web search for "abbreviations + Bible."

(Koran 18.65–82)

Speech, academic talk, or course lecture

Works Cited

Zien, Katherine. "Good Neighbor, Good Soldier: Staging Transhemispheric Militarization in the Former Panama Canal Zone." Paper presented at the ASTR/TLA Annual Conference, 4 Nov. 2016, Minneapolis Marriott City Center.

Speech, academic talk, or course lecture *(continued)*		Skeel, David. "Is Justice Possible?" Lecture, 13 Nov. 2014, U of Hong Kong. *YouTube*, uploaded by Faith HKU, 3 Dec. 2014, youtu .be/qeR_Y2KQTts. Doniger, Wendy. Course on evil in Hindu mythology. 15 Mar. 2007, U of Chicago. Lecture. ▸ You may indicate a live lecture or address, or another format that is not obvious, at the end of the reference.
	In-text	(Zien) (Skeel) (Doniger)
Personal communication or interview	Works Cited	▸ Personal communications can often be mentioned in the text alone. If you'd like to include them in the works cited list, they would look like this: Alter, Robert. Personal interview. 21 Oct. 2015. Sarkozy, Nicolas. Telephone interview. 5 May 2017. Lucas, George. Video interview, Skype. 18 Feb. 2010. Anonymous zzzzUS soldier, recently returned from Afghanistan. Personal interview. 28 Jan. 2014. Coates, Ta-Nehisi. "On Charlottesville, Trump, the Confederacy, Reparations & More." Interview by Amy Goodman and Juan González. *Democracy Now!*, 15 Aug. 2017, www.democracynow.org/2017/8/15/full _interview_ta_nehisi_coates_on. Rosenquist, James. "Reminiscing on the Gulf of Mexico: A Conversation with James Rosenquist." Interview by Jan van der Marck. *American Art*, vol. 20, no. 3, Fall 2006, pp. 84–107.
	In-text	(Alter) (Sarkozy) (Lucas) (anonymous US soldier) (Coates) (Rosenquist 93)

Poem	Works Cited	Auden, W. H. "The Shield of Achilles." 1952. *Collected Poems*, edited by Edward Mendelson, Random House, 2007, pp. 596–98.

▶ Auden's poem is dated 1952 by Mendelson. The original date of a poem in a collection or anthology is optional.

Robards, Brooks. "The Front." *On Island: Poems and Paintings of Martha's Vineyard*, Summerset Press, 2014, p. 17.

Balakian, Peter. "Near the Border." *Ozone Journal*, U of Chicago P, 2015, pp. 69–74.

Paredez, Deborah. "St. Joske's." 2012. *Poets. org*, www.poets.org/poetsorg/poem/st -joskes.

	In-text	(Auden 596) or (Auden, "Shield of Achilles" 596) or ("Shield of Achilles" 596) or (Auden 596; lines 9–11) or (Auden, lines 9–11) or (lines 9–11) or (9–11)

▶ Do not use abbreviations for "line" or "lines" since a lowercase *l* is easily confused with the number 1.

(Robards)

(Balakian 70) or (Balakian, "Near the Border" 70)

(Paredez) or (Paredez, "St. Joske's")

Play, text	Works Cited	Ruhl, Sarah. *Stage Kiss*. 2011. Theatre Communications Group, 2014.

▶ The play was first produced in 2011, published in 2014.

Shakespeare, William. *Romeo and Juliet*.

▶ If you wish to cite a specific edition:

Shakespeare, William. *Romeo and Juliet*. Edited by Brian Gibbons, Methuen, 1980.

▶ For an online version:

Shakespeare, William. *Romeo and Juliet*. Edited by William J. Rolfe, American Book, 1907. Project Gutenberg, www.gutenberg .org/files/47960/47960-h/47960-h.htm.

	In-text	(Ruhl) or (Ruhl, *Stage Kiss*)

(Shakespeare, *Romeo and Juliet* 1.3.12–15) or (*Romeo and Juliet* 1.3.12–15) or

Play, text *(continued)*		(1.3.12–15) if the play's name is clear in the text
		▸ This refers to act 1, scene 3, lines 12–15 (separated by periods).
		▸ If you refer repeatedly to Shakespeare's plays, you can use MLA's standard abbreviations for them, such as (*Ham.*) for *Hamlet*. The first time you mention a play such as *Romeo and Juliet*, you simply indicate the abbreviation (*Rom.*), and then use it after that for in-text citations, such as (*Rom.* 1.3.12–15).
Performance of play or dance	Works Cited	*Romeo and Juliet*. Choreography by Krzysztof Pastor, music by Sergei Prokofiev, Joffrey Ballet, 13 Oct. 2016, Auditorium Theatre, Chicago.
		The Rembrandt. Written by Jessica Dickey, directed by Hallie Gordon, performance by Francis Guinan and John Mahoney, 6 Oct. 2017, Steppenwolf Theatre, Chicago.
		▸ If you are concentrating on one person's work in theater, music, dance, or other collaborative arts, put that person's name first. For example, if you are focusing on Francis Guinan's acting:
		Guinan, Francis, performer. *The Rembrandt*. Written by Jessica Dickey, directed by Hallie Gordon, 6 Oct. 2017, Steppenwolf Theatre, Chicago.
	In-text	*(Romeo and Juliet)*
		(Rembrandt) or (Guinan)
Television program	Works Cited	"The Children." *Game of Thrones*, written by David Benioff and D. B. Weiss, directed by Alex Graves, season 4, episode 10, HBO, 15 June 2014.
		"Pressing the Flesh." *Scandal*, written by Shonda Rhimes, performance by Kerry Washington, Katie Lowes, and Scott Foley, season 7, episode 2, ABC, 12 Oct. 2017. Hulu, www.hulu.com/watch/1156610.
	In-text	("The Children")
		("Pressing the Flesh")

Film	Works Cited	*Godfather II*. Directed by Francis Ford Coppola, performance by Al Pacino, Robert De Niro, Robert Duvall, and Diane Keaton, screenplay by Francis Ford Coppola and Mario Puzo, based on the novel by Mario Puzo, Paramount Pictures, 1974. Paramount Home Video, Godfather DVD Collection, 2003.

▶ Optional information includes actors, producers, screenwriters, editors, cinematographers, etc. Include what you need for analysis in your paper, in order of their importance to your analysis. Their names appear between the title and the distributor.

▶ If you are concentrating on one person's work, put that person's name and role (such as performer) first, before the title:

Coppola, Francis Ford, director. *Godfather II*. Performance by Al Pacino, Robert De Niro, Robert Duvall, and Diane Keaton, Paramount Pictures, 1974. Paramount Home Video, Godfather DVD Collection, 2003.

Tig. Directed by Kristina Goolsby and Ashley York, Beachside / Netflix, 2015. Netflix, www.netflix.com/title/80028208.

▶ If there is more than one production company, list both with a slash between them. In the example above, Netflix is both a producer and the name of the website from which the film was retrieved.

	In-text	(*Godfather II*) or (Coppola) (*Tig*)

Artwork	Works Cited	Tintoretto, Jacopo Robusti. *The Birth of John the Baptist*. 1550s, State Hermitage Museum, St. Petersburg. Oil on canvas, 181 × 266 cm.

▶ The size and medium are optional.

Tintoretto, Jacopo Robusti. *The Birth of John the Baptist*. 1550s, State Hermitage Museum, St. Petersburg. *Tintoretto: Tradition and Identity*, by Tom Nichols, Reaktion Books, 1999, p. 47.

Artwork (*continued*)		▸ For a reproduction, cite where you found the work. Tintoretto, Jacopo Robusti. *The Birth of John the Baptist*. 1550s, State Hermitage Museum, St. Petersburg, www.hermitage-museum.org/wps/portal/hermitage/digital-collection/01.+Paintings/32113/?lng=en. ▸ Include a website and URL for artwork found online, but if the website and museum share the same name, there is no need to list both.
	In-text	(Tintoretto) or (Tintoretto, *Birth of John the Baptist*)
Photograph	Works Cited	Adams, Ansel. *Monolith, the Face of Half Dome, Yosemite National Park*. 1927, Art Institute, Chicago. Adams, Ansel. *Dunes, Oceano, California*. 1963. *MoMA*, www.moma.org/collection/works/58283.
	In-text	(Adams) or (Adams, *Monolith*) (Adams) or (Adams, *Dunes, Oceano*)
Figures: map, chart, graph, or table	Works Cited	Digout, Delphine. "Climate Change Vulnerability in Africa." Revised by Hugo Ahlenius, UNEP/GRID-Arendal, 2002. *GRID-Arendal*, old.grida.no/graphicslib/detail/climate-change-vulnerability-in-africa_7239. "Presidential Election Results: Donald J. Trump Wins." 9 Aug. 2017. *The New York Times*, www.nytimes.com/elections/results/president. Interactive map. ▸ If the format (here an interactive map) is not obvious from the title, you may specify the type of work. "1427 E. 60th St., Chicago IL 60637." *Google Maps*, www.google.com/maps/place/The+University+of+Chicago+Press,+1427+E+60th+St,+Chicago,+IL+60637/. Accessed 25 Oct. 2017. 2017. ▸ For undated maps consulted online, include an access date.

▶ A map published in a book or journal can usually be mentioned in the text (see "In-text," below); cite the work as a whole in the Works Cited list:

Menkhaus, Ken. "Governance without Government in Somalia: Spoilers, State Building, and the Politics of Coping." *International Security*, vol. 31, no. 7, Winter 2006/7, pp. 74–106.

In-text

("Climate Change Vulnerability in Africa") ("Presidential Election Results") ("Map of Somalia, 2006/7") or (Menkhaus 79, map)

Musical recording

Works Cited

Johnson, Robert. "Come On in My Kitchen (Take 1)." 1936. *Robert Johnson: King of the Delta Blues Singers*, expanded ed., Columbia/Legacy, 1998.

Johnson, Robert. "Traveling Riverside Blues." 1937. *Robert Johnson: King of the Delta Blues Singers*, Columbia Records 1654, 1961. LP.

Allman Brothers Band. "Come On in My Kitchen." Written by Robert Johnson, *Shades of Two Worlds*. Sony, 1991.

Barber, Samuel. Cello sonata, for cello and piano, op. 6. *Barber: Adagio for Strings, Violin Concerto, Orchestral and Chamber Works*, St. Louis Symphony, conducted by Leonard Slatkin, Alan Stepansky, cello, Israela Margalit, piano, EMI Classics 74287, 2001. CD.

▶ Catalog numbers can be listed with publication details to help readers locate a specific recording.

▶ If you consulted a physical medium, add it at the end of the entry.

▶ If you are concentrating on one person's work, such as the pianist, his or her name can come first:

Musical recording (*continued*)		Margalit, Israela, piano. Cello sonata, for cello and piano, op. 6. *Barber: Adagio for Strings, Violin Concerto, Orchestral and Chamber Works*, St. Louis Symphony, conducted by Leonard Slatkin, Alan Stepansky, cello, EMI Classics 74287, 2001. Beyoncé. "Formation." *Lemonade*, Parkwood Entertainment, 2016. ▶ You do not need to include the software application or website where you accessed the music. If you choose to do so, it would look like this: Beyoncé. "Formation." *Lemonade*, *iTunes* app, Parkwood Entertainment, 2016.
	In-text	(Johnson) or (Johnson, "Come") (Johnson) or (Johnson, "Traveling") (Allman Brothers) or (Allman Brothers, "Come") (Barber) or (Barber, Cello sonata) (Margalit) or (Margalit, Cello sonata) (Beyoncé) or (Beyoncé, "Formation")
Music video	Works Cited	Arcade Fire. *Everything Now. YouTube*, uploaded by ArcadeFireVEVO, 1 June 2017, youtu.be/zC3oBYR3CUk. Rihanna et al. *FourFiveSeconds*. Directed by Inez & Vinoodh, produced by Stephanie Bargas and Jeff Lepine. *Vevo*, 3 Feb. 2015, www.vevo.com/watch/rihanna/fourfive seconds/QMFUA1590146. Video. ▶ You can specify "Video" if it's not clear from the entry. ▶ Do not include comments on videos (or any web content) in the works cited list.
	In-text	(Arcade Fire) or (Arcade Fire, *Everything Now*) (Rihanna et al.)
Sheet music	Works Cited	Bach, Johann Sebastian. *Toccata and Fugue in D Minor*. 1708. BWV 565, arranged by Ferruccio Benvenuto Busoni for solo piano, G. Schirmer LB1629, 1942.

		▶ This piece was written in 1708 and has the standard Bach classification BWV 565. The arrangement is published by G. Schirmer, with its catalog number LB1629.
	In-text	(*Toccata and Fugue in D Minor*) or (Bach, *Toccata and Fugue in D Minor*)
Liner notes	Works Cited	Reich, Steven. Liner notes. *Different Trains*. Kronos Quartet, Elektra/Nonesuch 9 79176-2, 1988. CD.
	In-text	(Reich, *Different Trains*)
Audiobook	Works Cited	Eliot, George. *Middlemarch*. Narrated by Juliet Stevenson, Audible, 2011. Audiobook.
	In-text	(Eliot) or (Eliot, *Middlemarch*) or (Eliot 01:02:20–27) ▶ To cite a specific part of the text, refer to the time or range of time in the in-text citation.
Advertisement	Works Cited	Advertisement for *Letters from Iwo Jima*. *The New York Times*, 6 Feb. 2007, p. B4. Advertisement for Vitamin Water. *Rolling Stone*, 15 June 2017, p. 17. "Be a Mindsticker," advertisement for Tab cola. Coca-Cola Co., circa late 1960s. *Dailymotion*, 8 Aug. 2007, www.dailymotion.com/video/x2s3qd.
	In-text	(*Letters from Iwo Jima* advertisement) (Vitamin Water advertisement) (Tab advertisement)
Government document	Works Cited	United States, Congress, Senate, Committee on Armed Services. *Hearings on S. 758, a Bill to Promote the National Security by Providing for a National Defense Establishment.* Government Printing Office, 1947. 80th Congress, 1st session, Senate Report 239. United States, Congress, House. *American Health Care Act. Congress.gov*, 2017, www.congress.gov/bill/115th-congress/house-bill/1628/text.

Government
document
(*continued*)

▸ Number and session of Congress, chamber, and type and number of publication are optional.

United States, Environmental Protection Agency, Office of Air and Radiation. *A Brief Guide to Mold, Moisture, and Your Home.* EPA.gov, 2012, www.epa.gov/mold/brief -guide-mold-moisture-and-your-home.

Freedman, Stephen. *Four-Year Impacts of Ten Programs on Employment Stability and Earnings Growth: The National Evalua- tion of Welfare-to-Work Strategies.* US Department of Education, 2000, www .mdrc.org/publication/four-year-impacts -ten-programs-employment-stability-and -earnings-growth.

United States, Department of State. Daily Press Briefing. US Department of State, 9 Aug. 2017, www.state.gov/r/pa/prs/dpb/2017/ 08/273288.htm.

In-text

(US Cong., Senate, Committee on Armed Services)

▸ If you are referencing only one item from that committee, then in-text citations don't need to include the hearing number or report.

(US Cong., Senate, Committee on Armed Ser- vices, *Hearings on S. 758*, 1947)

▸ If you refer to several items from the commit- tee, indicate which one you are citing. You can shorten that after the first use:

(*Hearings on S. 758*)

(US, EPA, Office of Air and Radiation 15)

(Freedman 6) or (Freedman, *Four-Year Impacts*)

(US Dept. of State) or (US Dept. of State, *Press Briefing*, 9 Aug. 2017)

Website, page
or entire

Works Cited

"News and Advocacy." *American Historical Association*, www.historians.org/news-and -advocacy. Accessed 9 Nov. 2017.

de Blasio, Bill. "State of the City 2017." *Office of the Mayor*, City of New York, 13 Feb. 2017, www1.nyc.gov/office-of-the-mayor/state-of -our-city.page.

Lipson, Charles. "News and Commentary:
US and the World." *Charles Lipson*, www
.charleslipson.com/News-links.htm.
Accessed 29 Aug. 2017.

▸ For webpages without identifiable authors,
begin the citation with the title of the page or
website.

▸ If there is no date of publication, posting, or
revision, include an access date.

▸ Webpages and other online documents may
not have numbered pages. You may, however,
be able to cite to a specific section (Lipson,
sec. 7) or paragraph (Lipson, pars. 3–5).

In-text	("News and Advocacy") (de Blasio) or (de Blasio, "State of the City") (Lipson)

Blog, post or comment	Works Cited	Jayson, Sharon. "Is Selfie Culture Making Our Kids Selfish?" *Well*, *The New York Times*, 23 June 2016, well.blogs.nytimes.com/ 2016/06/23/is-selfie-culture-making-our -kids-selfish. Arana, Ana. "The Deep Magic of Mexico." *The Big Roundtable*, 8 Dec. 2016, thebiground table.com/the-deep-magic-of-mexico -2bf1b341d1a1. ▸ Blog posts (or entries) are cited like articles from newspapers or news sites. Cheryl. Comment on "Is Selfie Culture Mak-ing Our Kids Selfish?" *Well*, *The New York Times*, 23 June 2016, well.blogs.nytimes .com/2016/06/23/is-selfie-culture-making -our-kids-selfish.
	In-text	(Jayson) or (Jayson, "Selfie Culture") (Arana) or (Arana, "Deep Magic")

Video	Works Cited	*Duck and Cover.* Archer Productions / Federal Civil Defense Administration, 1951. *You-Tube*, uploaded by Nuclear Vault, 11 July 2009, youtu.be/IKqXu-5jw6o. ▸ This 1951 film was posted online in 2009.

Video (*continued*)		"Jury Convicts Martin Shkreli on Three Counts of Security Fraud." *NBC*, 4 Aug. 2017, www.nbcnews.com/video/jury-convicts-martin-shkreli-on-three-counts-of-securities-fraud-1017719875664. Wang, Tricia. "The Human Insights Missing from Big Data." *TED*, Sept. 2016, www.ted.com/talks/tricia_wang_the_human_insights_missing_from_big_data. Video. ▸ You can specify "Video" if it's not clear from the entry. ▸ Why is *Duck and Cover* in italics but "Jury Convicts Martin Shkreli" and "Human Insights" placed in quotation marks? Because MLA italicizes films and TV series but "quotes" individual episodes. The emergence of new media blurs this once-bright line. In this case, *Duck and Cover* is italicized because it was produced as a stand-alone film, albeit a brief one. The two other examples, on the other hand, are more like individual episodes in a series.
	In-text	(*Duck and Cover*) ("Jury")
Multimedia app (video game, other stand-alone application)	Works Cited	*Madden NFL 18*. Standard ed., EA Sports, 25 Aug. 2017. ▸ Include any other information you think is relevant: *Madden NFL 18*. EA Sports, PlayStation 4, Nov. 2017. *Geocaching*. Groundspeak, v. 5.6.1, 2017.
	In-text	(*Madden NFL 18*) (*Geocaching*)
Podcast	Works Cited	"Has Anybody Called You?" *S-Town*, ch. 2, hosted by Brian Reed, produced by Brian Reed and Julie Snyder, Serial Productions, 28 Mar. 2017, stownpodcast.org/chapter/2. ▸ or Reed, Brian, host. "Has Anybody Called You?" *S-Town*, ch. 2, produced by Brian Reed and Julie Snyder, Serial Productions, 28 Mar. 2017, stownpodcast.org/chapter/2.

DeGeneres, Ellen. "Ellen's Parenting Advice."
The Ellen Show Podcast, Telepictures Productions, 26 June 2015, *iTunes*.

In-text   ("Has Anybody Called You?") or (Reed)
(DeGeneres) or (DeGeneres, "Ellen's Parenting
Advice")

Social media   Works Cited   Zuckerberg, Mark. Profile. *Facebook*, www
(Facebook,   .facebook.com/zuck.
Instagram,   Tyson, Neil deGrasse (@neiltyson). "Always
Twitter)   seemed to me that millipedes have more
legs than are necessary." *Twitter*, 7 July
2017, 1:25 p.m., twitter.com/neiltyson/
status/883421859072458752.

▸ For the title, use the text of the post, up to 160
characters.

Chicago Manual of Style. "Is the world ready
for singular they? We thought so back
in 1993." *Facebook*, 17 Apr. 2015, www
.facebook.com/ChicagoManual/posts/
10152906193679151.

Richards, Corey (@coryrichards). "A quiet if not
solemn day on Everest." *Instagram*, 24 May
2017, www.instagram.com/p/BUekBZLg
DOW/.

▸ Publicly available social media content should
be cited this way. Private content such as direct
messages should be cited like text messages.

In-text   (Zuckerberg)
(Tyson)
(Chicago Manual of Style)
(Richards) or (Richards, "Quiet")

Email, texts   Works Cited   ▸ Texts and other personal messages can often be
(direct   cited in the text alone. If you'd like to include
messages)   them in the works cited list, they'd look like
this:

Leis, Kathy. "Re: New Orleans family." Received
by Karen Turkish, 3 Mar. 2017.

▸ For title, use the subject of the email.

Lipson, Michael. *Facebook* message to Jona-
than Lipson. 9 Feb. 2016.

Email, texts (direct messages) (*continued*)		► Include the time for instant messages or emails if they are pertinent. For example: 9 Feb. 2010, 3:15 p.m.
	In-text	(Leis) (Lipson) or (Lipson, M.)
Electronic forum or mailing list	Works Cited	Polger, Mark Aaron. "CALL: Call for Proposals." American Library Association mailing list archives, ACRL Campaign for Libraries list, 10 May 2017, lists.ala.org/sympa/arc/academicpr/2017-05/msg00005.html. Ngo, Quinn. "Re: What Are Some Unknown Truths about College Life?" *Quora*, 14 July 2017, www.quora.com/What-are-some-unknown-truths-about-college-life.
	In-text	(Polger) (Ngo)

A lot of terms that used to be abbreviated in MLA style can now be spelled out, but some things are still usually abbreviated. For example, terms like *editor* are now spelled out, but *edition* is always abbreviated. All months are shortened, except May, June, and July. Here are some other examples:

MLA: COMMON ABBREVIATIONS

and others	et al.	note	n	pseudonym	pseud.
appendix	app.	notes	nn	University [as part	U
book	bk.	number	no.	of a proper noun]	
chapter	ch.	opus	op.	University Press	UP
compare	cf.	opuses	opp.	verse	v.
document	doc.	page	p.	verses	vv.
edition	ed.	pages	pp.	versus	vs.
especially	esp.	paragraph	par.	volume	vol.
figure	fig.	part	pt.		
library	lib.	press	p		

Note: All abbreviations (except for those that shorten publisher names) are lowercase, usually followed by a period. Most form their plurals by adding *s*.
The exceptions are note (n → nn), opus (op. → opp.), page (p. → pp.), and translator (same abbreviation).

In citing poetry, do not use abbreviations for "line" or "lines" since a lowercase *l* is easily confused with the number 1. Use either the full word or, if the meaning is clear, simply the number.

In publishers' names, in addition to using the abbreviations U, P, and UP, you can usually omit words and abbreviations like Company, Co., and Inc.

FAQS ABOUT MLA CITATIONS

What's the deal with MLA's "containers"?

Container is just another name for "facts of publication." Most entries in your Works Cited will include an author, a title, and certain facts of publication. (Each of these three categories ends with a period; commas separate items within each category.) These facts consist of information about the work—for example, the publisher and date for a book, or the name of the series and other relevant info for a TV episode.

Sometimes a second container is needed—for example, for a book or a show that you read or watched online. In that case, after the usual facts (the first container, which is followed by a period), you would add the name of the website and a URL.

Not all works found online require a second container. For example, a news article from the *Los Angeles Times* online needs only one, because the name of the newspaper and the website that publishes it are the same.

You'll find lots of examples above.

How do I handle the citation when one author quotes another?

That happens frequently, as in Donald Kagan's book *The Peloponnesian War*, which often quotes Thucydides. Using MLA style, you might write:

> Kagan approvingly quotes Thucydides, who says that Athens acquired this vital site "because of the hatred they already felt toward the Spartans" (quoted in Kagan 14).

In your Works Cited, you include Kagan but *not* Thucydides for this particular quote. You would include the ancient Greek historian in Works Cited only if you quoted him directly elsewhere in your paper.

5 APA CITATIONS FOR THE SOCIAL SCIENCES, EDUCATION, AND BUSINESS

APA citations are widely used in psychology, education, business, and the social sciences. (Some engineering students are also required to use APA, but most use IEEE or ACSE, which are discussed in chapter 11.) Like MLA citations, APA citations are in text. Notes are used only for analysis and commentary, not to cite references. Unlike MLA, however, APA emphasizes the year of publication, which comes immediately after the author's name. That's probably because as scholarship cumulates in the sciences and empirical social sciences (where APA is used), it is important to know whether the research was conducted recently and whether it came before or after other research. At least that's the rationale.

Detailed information on the APA system is available in the *Publication Manual of the American Psychological Association*, 6th ed. (2010), and *APA Style Guide to Electronic Resources*, 6th ed. (2012).

To get started, let's look at APA references for a journal article, a chapter in an edited book, and a book as they appear at the end of a paper. APA calls this a "Reference List." (MLA calls it "Works Cited," and Chicago calls it "Bibliography.")

> Lipson, C. (1991). Why are some international agreements informal? *International Organization, 45*, 495–538.
> Lipson, C. (1994). Is the future of collective security like the past? In G. Downs (Ed.), *Collective security beyond the cold war* (pp. 105–131). Ann Arbor: University of Michigan Press.
> Lipson, C. (2003). *Reliable partners: How democracies have made a separate peace*. Princeton, NJ: Princeton University Press.

This list for the distinguished author C. Lipson follows another APA rule. All entries for a single author are arranged by year of publication, beginning with the earliest. If there were two entries for a particular year, say 2018, they would be alphabetized by title and the first would be labeled (2018a), the second (2018b). A future publication would be cited as "(in press)." Also note the APAs rules for capitalizing book and article titles. They are treated like sentences, with only the first words capitalized. If there's a colon in the title, the first word after the colon is also capitalized. Proper nouns are capitalized, of course, just as they are in sentences.

In these reference lists, single-author entries precede those with coauthors. So Pinker, S. (as a sole author) would precede Pinker, S., & Jones, B. In the APA system, multiple authors are joined by an ampersand "&" rather than the word *and*. It is not clear why. Just accept it as a rule, like how many minutes are in a soccer game.

The authors' first names are always reduced to initials. That makes APA different from MLA and Chicago, as does its frequent use of commas and parentheses.

When works are cited in the text, the citation includes the author's name unless the author's name has already been mentioned in that sentence. For instance:

These claims are backed up by the most recent data (Nye, 2018).

If the sentence includes the author's name, the citation omits it. For instance:

Nye (2018) presents considerable data to back up his claims.

If you include a direct quote, then you *must* include the page number in the citation. For instance:

"The policy is poorly conceived," according to Nye (2018, p. 12).

The examples in this chapter focus on psychology, education, other social sciences, and business, where APA citations are most widely used, just as the MLA examples focus on the humanities, where that style is common.

To make it easy to find the types of APA citations you need, I've listed them here alphabetically, along with the pages where they are described. At the end of the chapter I have listed some common APA abbreviations.

INDEX OF APA CITATIONS IN THIS CHAPTER

APA: REFERENCE LIST AND IN-TEXT CITATIONS

Book, one
author

Reference list

King, B. J. (2017). *Personalities on the plate: The lives and minds of animals we eat.* Chicago, IL: University of Chicago Press.

▸ APA requires the state even for well-known cities. Exception: if the name of a university publisher includes the state, you can omit it (e.g., Ann Arbor: University of Michigan Press).

Naughton, B. (2007). *The Chinese economy: Transitions and growth.* Cambridge, MA: MIT Press.

Fitzpatrick, M. (2017). *Invisible scars: Mental trauma and the Korean War.* Vancouver, British Columbia, Canada: University of British Columbia Press.

▸ Although US states are abbreviated, Canadian provinces and territories are spelled out and the country name is included.

	In-text	(King, 2017) (Naughton, 2007) (Fitzpatrick, 2017)

Books and articles, several by same author	Reference list	Posner, R. C. (2007a). *Countering terrorism.* Lanham, MD: Rowman & Littlefield with the Hoover Institution. Posner, R. C. (2007b). *Economic analysis of law* (7th ed.). New York, NY: Aspen Law and Business. Posner, R. C. (2007c). *The little book of plagiarism.* New York, NY: Pantheon. Posner, R. C. (2006a). *Not a suicide pact: The Constitution in a time of national emergency.* New York, NY: Oxford University Press. Posner, R. C. (2006b). *Uncertain shield: The U.S. intelligence system in the throes of reform.* Lanham, MD: Rowman & Littlefield with the Hoover Institution. Posner R. C., & Becker, G. S. (2006). *Suicide and risk-taking: An economic approach.* Unpublished paper, University of Chicago.

▶ Note that the author's name is repeated. APA does not use dashes for repetition.

▶ When the same author or coauthors have several publications in the same year, list them alphabetically (by the first significant word in the title). Label them as "a," "b," and "c." The last 2006 item by Posner is *not* labeled "c" because its authorship is different.

▶ Coauthored books like Posner & Becker follow a writer's single-author ones, in the alphabetical order of the second author's surname.

	In-text	(Posner, 2007a, 2007b, 2007c, 2006a, 2006b; Posner & Becker, 2006)

Book, multiple authors	Reference list	Gazzaley, A., & Rosen, L.D. (2016). *The distracted mind: Ancient brains in a high-tech world.* Cambridge, MA: MIT Press.

Book, multiple authors (*continued*)		Useem, M., Singh, H., Neng, L., & Cappelli, P. (2017). *Fortune makers: The leaders creating China's great global companies.* New York, NY: Public Affairs.

Butcher, T., Guo, X., Harris, J., Lette, K., Mankell, H., Moggach, D., . . . Welsh, I. (2010). *Because I'm a girl.* New York, NY: Random House.

> ▸ Name up to seven authors; for eight or more, list the first six followed by an ellipsis (three spaced periods) and then the name of the last author.

In-text

(Gazzaley & Rosen, 2016)
(Useem, Singh, Neng, & Cappelli, 2017), and then (Useem et al., 2017)

> ▸ For two authors, always list both. For three to five authors, name all authors in the first citation. Beginning with the second reference, name only the first author, then add "et al.": (Fubini et al., 2007)
> ▸ For six or more authors, name only the first author, then add "et al." for all citations.
> ▸ Use "&" within parenthetical references but not in the text itself.

Book, multiple editions

Reference list

DiClemente, C. C. (2018). *Addiction and change: How addictions develop and addicted people recover* (2nd ed.). New York, NY: Guilford Press.

> ▸ If it says "revised edition" rather than "2nd edition," use "(Rev. ed.)" in the same spot.

Strunk, W., Jr., & White, E. B. (2009). *The elements of style* (50th anniversary ed.). New York, NY: Longman.

In-text

(Strunk & White, 2009)

> ▸ To refer to a specific page for a quotation: (Strunk & White, 2009, p. 12)

Book, corporate author or no author

Reference list

University of Michigan, Office of Student Publications. (2017). *2017 alumni directory.* Bloomington, IN: University Publishing Corporation.

American Psychological Association. (2010). *Publication manual of the American Psychological Association* (6th ed.). Washington, DC: Author.

▸ If the publisher is the same as the author, write "Author" in place of the former.

The bluebook: A uniform system of citation (20th ed.). (2015). Cambridge, MA: Harvard Law Review Association.

▸ For multiple editions without authors, the form is *Title* (edition). (year). City, STATE: Publisher.

In-text

(University of Michigan, 2017)

▸ Abbreviate a corporate author on subsequent mentions only, and only if the abbreviation will be immediately recognizable to readers.

(American Psychological Association [APA], 2010)

▸ Subsequent references are (APA, 2010) or (*Bluebook*, 2015).

Book, edited

Reference list

Bakker, K. (Ed.). (2007). *Eau Canada: The future of Canada's water*. Vancouver, British Columbia, Canada: University of British Columbia Press.

Bosworth, M., & Flavin, J. (Eds.). (2007). *Race, gender, and punishment: From colonialism to the war on terror*. New Brunswick, NJ: Rutgers University Press.

Matthijs, M., & Blyth, M. (Eds.). (2015). *The future of the Euro*. Oxford, England: Oxford University Press.

In-text

(Bakker, 2007)
(Bosworth & Flavin, 2007)
(Matthijs & Blyth 2015)

E-book

Reference list

Toy, E. C., & Klamen, D. (2015). *Case files: Psychiatry* (5th ed.) [Kindle Fire HDX version]. Retrieved from http://www.amazon.com

E-book *(continued)*		► APA says to put important but "nonroutine" information in square brackets following the title (and after any parenthetical information—about edition, volumes, etc.). ► Electronic retrieval information takes the place of the publisher location and name. That's code for URL. If the URL is very long, cite the home page (as in this example).
	In-text	(Toy & Klamen, 2015)
Book, online	Reference list	Reed, J. (1922). *Ten days that shook the world* [Etext 3076]. Retrieved from http://www.gutenberg.org/dirs/etext02/10daz10.txt ► APA does *not* put a period after the URL, making it different from most other reference styles. ► And APA does *not* want access dates—except for sources that may change over time (think *Wikipedia* article).
	In-text	(Reed, 1922)
Multivolume work	Reference list	Rothschild, B. (2017). *The body remembers* (Vols. 1–2). New York, NY: Norton. Pflanze, O. (1963–1990). *Bismarck and the development of Germany* (Vols. 1–3). Princeton, NJ: Princeton University Press.
	In-text	(Rothschild, 2017) (Pflanze, 1963–1990)
Single volume in a multivolume work	Reference list	Rothschild, B. (2017). *The body remembers: Vol. 2. Revolutionizing trauma treatment.* New York, NY: Norton. Pflanze, O. (1990). *Bismarck and the development of Germany: Vol. 3. The period of fortification, 1880–1898.* Princeton, NJ: Princeton University Press.
	In-text	(Rothschild, 2017) (Pflanze, 1990)

Reprint of earlier edition	Reference list	Smith, A. (1976). *An inquiry into the nature and causes of the wealth of nations.* E. Cannan (Ed.). Chicago, IL: University of Chicago Press. (Original work published 1776) ▸ There is no period after the parenthesis.
	In-text	(Smith, 1776/1976)
Translated volume	Reference list	Weber, M. (1958). *The Protestant ethic and the spirit of capitalism.* T. Parsons (Trans.). New York, NY: Charles Scribner's Sons. (Original work published 1904–1905)
	In-text	(Weber, 1904–1905/1958)
Foreign-language volume	Reference list	Weber, M. (2005). *Die protestantische Ethik und der Geist des Kapitalismus* [The Protestant ethic and the spirit of capitalism]. Erftstadt, Germany: Area Verlag. (Original work published 1904–1905)
	In-text	(Weber, 1904–1905/2005)
Chapter in edited book	Reference list	Board, J. (2016). The paradox of right and wrong. In R. Bolden, M. Witzel, & N. Linacre (Eds.), *Leadership paradoxes: Rethinking leadership for an uncertain world* (pp. 131–150). New York, NY: Routledge. ▸ Chapter titles are not in quotes or italics.
	In-text	(Board, 2016)
Journal article, one author	Reference list	Ivanov, M. (2016). Dynamic learning and strategic communication. *International Journal of Game Theory, 45,* 627–653. https://doi.org/10.1007/s00182-015-0474-x Massaro, D. W. (2017). Reading aloud to children: Benefits and implications for acquiring literacy before schooling begins. *The American Journal of Psychology, 130,* 63–72. https://doi.org/10.5406/amerjpsyc.130.1.0063

Journal article, one author (*continued*)		Wettersten, J. (2014). New social tasks for cognitive psychology; or, new cognitive tasks for social psychology [Abstract]. *American Journal of Pyschology, 127,* 403. http://www.jstor.org/stable/10.5406/amerjpsyc.127.4.0403

- ▸ Article titles are not in quotes or italics.
- ▸ The journal's volume number is italicized, but the issue number and pages are not. The word *volume* (or "Vol.") is omitted.
- ▸ There's no need to name a specific issue if the journal pages are numbered continuously throughout the year. However, if each issue begins with page 1, then the issue's number or month is necessary to find the article: *45*(2), 15–30.
- ▸ To cite an abstract, include "Abstract" in brackets after the article title.
- ▸ Include a Digital Object Identifier (DOI) for every journal article that has one—even if you're citing print. A URL based on a DOI (appended to https://doi.org/) is preferable to another kind of URL. If you're citing an article online and don't see a DOI, list the URL of the journal's home page or the database where you found it.

Mitchell, T. (2002). McJihad: Islam in the U.S. global order. *Social Text, 20*(4), 1–18. https://doi.org/10.1215/01642472-20-4_73-1

- ▸ The issue number (4, in parentheses but not in italics) is included because each issue of this journal starts over at page 1.

In-text	(Ivanov, 2016) (Massaro, 2017) (Wettersten, 2014) (Mitchell, 2002)

Journal article, multiple authors	Reference list	Lanis, R., Richardson, G., & Taylor, G. (2017). Board of director gender and corporate tax aggressiveness: An empirical analysis. *Journal of Business Ethics, 144,* 577–596. https://doi.org/10.1007/s10551-015-2815-x

Guo, S., Chen, D., Zhou, D., Sun, H., Wu, G., Haile, C., . . . Zhang, X. (2007). Association of functional catechol O-methyl transferase (COMT) Val108Met polymorphism with smoking severity and age of smoking initiation in Chinese male smokers. *Psychopharmacology, 190,* 449–456. https://doi.org/10.1007/s00213-006 -0628-4

▶ Name up to seven authors; for eight or more, list the first six followed by an ellipsis and then the last author's name.

In-text

(Lanis, Richardson, & Taylor, 2017) for first reference.
(Lanis et al., 2017) for second reference and after.

▶ When a work has three to five authors, name all of them in the first textual reference. After that, use only the first author's name plus "et al."
(Guo et al., 2007)

▶ When a work has six authors or more, name only the first one plus "et al." For example, this would be the first mention of the Guo article:
In their study of Chinese male smokers, Guo et al. (2007) find an association . . .

Journal article, foreign language

Reference list

Maignan, I., & Swaen, V. (2004). La responsabilité sociale d'une organisation: Intégration des perspectives marketing et managériale. *Revue Française du Marketing, 200,* 51–66.

▶ or

Maignan, I., & Swaen, V. (2004). La responsabilité sociale d'une organisation: Intégration des perspectives marketing et managériale [The social responsibility of an organization: Integration of marketing and managerial perspectives]. *Revue Française du Marketing, 200,* 51–66.

In-text

(Maignan & Swaen, 2004)

Newspaper or magazine article, with author	Reference list	Wingfield, N. (2017, September 11). The robots of Amazon. *The New York Times* (New York ed.), p. B1. ▸ APA includes an initial *The* in newspaper and magazine titles. ▸ Newspaper page numbers include "p." or "pp." Tsukayama, H. (2017, September 11). The iPhone is 10. Where does Apple go from here? *The Chicago Tribune*. Retrieved from www.chicagotribune.com Pandey, S. (2007, February 11). I read the news today, oh boy. *The Los Angeles Times* (Home ed.), p. M6. Retrieved from http://www.proquest.com ▸ Provide the URL for the homepage of the newspaper, magazine, or database, rather than the URL for the specific article.
	In-text	(Wingfield, 2017) or, if necessary, (Wingfield, September 11, 2017) (Tsukayama, 2017) or (Tsukayama, 2017, September 11) (Pandey, 2007) or (Pandey, 2007, February 11)
Newspaper or magazine article, no author	Reference list	Retired U.S. general is focus of inquiry over Iran leak. (2013, June 28). *The New York Times* (New York ed.), p. A18. America and China talk climate change: Heating up or cooling down? (2009, June 11). *The Economist 391* (8635), 61. ▸ APA treats magazines much like journals. If you can't determine the volume and issue numbers, leave them out and put "p." or "pp." before the page number(s).
	In-text	("Retired U.S. general," 2013) ("Climate change," 2009)
Review	Reference list	Pugh, A. J. (2014, May). [Review of the book *The gender trap: Parents and the pitfalls of raising boys and girls*, by E. W. Kane]. *American Journal of Sociology 119*, 1773–1775.

Vimercati, G. (2017, August 20). Soviet pseudoscience: The history of mind control [Review of the book *Homo Sovieticus: Brain waves, mind control, and telepathic destiny*, by W. Velminski]. *Los Angeles Review of Books*. Retrieved from https://lareviewofbooks.org/.

In-text	(Pugh, 2014)
	(Vimercati, 2017)

Unpublished paper, poster session, dissertation, or thesis

Reference list

Tang, S. (2017, February). *Profit driven team grouping in social networks*. Paper presented at the Thirty-First AAAI Conference on Artificial Intelligence, San Francisco.

► Only the month and year are needed for papers.

Tomz, M., & Van Houweling, R. P. (2009, August). *Candidate inconsistency and voter choice*. Unpublished manuscript, Stanford University and University of California, Berkeley. Retrieved from http://www.stanford.edu/~tomz/working/TomzVanHouweling-2009-08.pdf

► Other categories include "Manuscript submitted for publication" and "Manuscript in preparation."

Noble, L. (2006). *One goal, multiple strategies: Engagement in Sino-American WTO accession negotiations*. Unpublished master's thesis, University of British Columbia, Vancouver, Canada.

► APA considers any thesis or dissertation that's not available from a commercial database to be unpublished.

Sierra, L. M. (2013). *Indigenous neighborhood residents in the urbanization of La Paz, Bolivia, 1910–1950* (Doctoral dissertation, State University of New York at Binghamton). Retrieved from ProQuest Dissertations and Theses (UMI No. 3612828).

► That parenthetical string of letters and numbers at the end is the accession number—helpful in finding the item in the database.

Unpublished paper, poster session, dissertation, or thesis *(continued)*		‣ APA doesn't require the name of the institution for a thesis or dissertation retrieved from a commercial database, but why not add it anyway?
	In-text	(Tang, 2017) (Tomz & Van Houweling, 2009) (Noble, 2006) (Sierra, 2013)
Preprint	Reference list	Piatti, A. E. (2017). *On the extended stellar structure around NGC 288* [Preprint]. Retrieved from https://arxiv.org/pdf/1709.07284v1.pdf ‣ arXiv is a collection facility for scientific "e-prints." Some of them have been published and some have not. APA recommends updating your references when you're close to finishing your paper; if you've cited a preprint that's since been published, cite the published journal article. ‣ The title is in italics because it hasn't yet been accepted in a journal, and is therefore considered a stand-alone work. ‣ Some journals publish articles online ahead of time. You can cite these in one of two ways (and again, update the reference when the article gets published): Ravigné, V., Dieckmann, U., & Olivieri, I. (2009). Live where you thrive: Joint evolution of habitat choice and local adaptation facilitates specialization and promotes diversity. *The American Naturalist.* Advance online publication. https://doi.org/10.1086/605369 ‣ or Ravigné, V., Dieckmann, U., & Olivieri, I. (in press). Live where you thrive: Joint evolution of habitat choice and local adaptation facilitates specialization and promotes diversity. *The American Naturalist, 174,* E141–E169. https://doi.org/10.1086/605369

In-text	(Piatti, 2017) (Ravigné, Dieckmann, & Olivieri, 2009) or (Ravigné, Dieckmann, & Olivieri, in press) ▶ Subsequent references are (Ravigné et al., 2009) or (Ravigné et al., in press)

| Research
or technical
report,
policy paper,
other "gray
literature" | Reference list | Environmental Protection Agency. (2016,
December). *State of the science white*
paper: A summary of literature on the
chemical toxicity of plastics pollution to
aquatic life and aquatic-dependent wild-
life [White paper]. Retrieved from https://
www.epa.gov/sites/production/files/
2016-12/documents/plastics-aquatic-life
-report.pdf
Tarullo, D. (2017, October). *Monetary policy*
without a working theory of inflation.
[Working paper]. Retrieved from Hutchins
Center on Fiscal & Monetary Policy,
Brookings Institute website: https://www
.brookings.edu/research/monetary-policy
-without-a-working-theory-of-inflation/ |
| | In-text | (Environmental Protection Agency, 2016)
(Tarullo, 2017) |

| Encyclopedia
and dictionary | Reference list | Balkans: History. (1987). In *Encyclopaedia*
Britannica (15th ed., Vol. 14, pp. 570–588).
Chicago, IL: Encyclopaedia Britannica.
Balkans. (2017). *Encyclopaedia Britannica*
online. Retrieved from https://www
.britannica.com/place/Balkans
App. (2016, April 6). *Merriam-Webster*.
Retrieved from http://www.merriam
-webster.com/dictionary/app
Protest, *v*. (1971). *Compact edition of the*
Oxford English dictionary (Vol. 2, p. 2335).
Oxford, England: Oxford University Press.
▶ The word *protest* is both a noun and a verb.
Here I am citing the verb.
Graham, G. (2015). Behaviorism. In E. N.
Zalta (Ed.), *The Stanford encyclopedia of*
philosophy. Retrieved from http://plato
.stanford.edu/entries/behaviorism/ |

Encyclopedia and dictionary (*continued*)		Emotion. (n.d.). *Wikipedia*. Retrieved November 8, 2017, from http://en.wikipedia.org/ wiki/Emotion
		▸ Though APA does not recommend access dates for most types of sources, they do recommend them for undated sources that are subject to frequent updates—like this *Wikipedia* article.
	In-text	(Balkans: History, 1987)
		▸ You may wish to include the subtitle, "History," in this case to help the reader if the main article is long or if you are citing several articles with similar titles and dates.
		(Balkans, 2017)
		(App, 2016)
		(Protest, 1971)
		(Graham, 2015)
		(Emotion, n.d.)
Bible, Qur'an (Koran)	Reference list	▸ Not needed, except to reference a particular version.
		The five books of Moses: A translation with commentary. (2004). Robert Alter (Trans. & Ed.). New York, NY: Norton.
	In-text	Deut. 1:2 (New Revised Standard Version).
		▸ List the version you are using the first time it is mentioned in the text. After that, omit the version.
		Gen. 1:1, 1:3–5, 2:4.
		▸ Books of the Bible can be abbreviated: Exod., Lev., Num., Cor., and so on.
		Qur'an 18:65–82.
Classical works	Reference list	▸ Not needed, except to reference a particular version.
		Plato. (2006). *The republic*. R. E. Allen (Trans.). New Haven, CT: Yale University Press. (Original work, approximately 360 BC)

Virgil. (2017). *The Aeneid*. D. Ferry (Trans.). Chicago, IL: University of Chicago Press. (Original work, approximately 19–29 BC)

In-text (Plato, trans. 2006)
(Virgil, trans. 2017)

Speech, academic talk, or course lecture	Reference list	Wingfield, A. M. H. (2016, August 21. Presidential address at the annual meeting of the American Sociological Association, Seattle, WA. Rector, N. (2017, March 6). Course lecture at the University of Toronto, Toronto, Ontario, Canada. Shiller, R.J. (2011). Risk and financial crisis. [recorded lecture]. Retrieved from http://oyc.yale.edu/economics/econ-252-11/lecture-2
	In-text	(Wingfield, 2016) (Rector, 2017) (Shiller, 2011)
Personal communication or interview	Reference list	Gates, B. (2014, March 13). Bill Gates: the Rolling Stone interview. (J. Goodell, Interviewer). Retrieved from http://www.rollingstone.com/culture/news/bill-gates-the-rolling-stone-interview-20140313 Smith, H. (1941). Interview by J. H. Faulk [Audio file]. Library of Congress, Archive of Folk Culture, American Folklife Center, Washington, DC. Retrieved from http://hdl.loc.gov/loc.afc/afc9999001.5499a
	In-text	(Gates, 2014) (Smith, 1941) (J. M. Coetzee, personal interview, May 5, 2017) (D. A. Grossberg, personal communication, January 1, 2015) (anonymous US soldier, recently returned from Afghanistan, interviewed by author, August 22, 2010)

Personal communication or interview (*continued*)		▸ The reference list includes published or archived interviews, like Gates's and Smith's, but not personal communications such as private conversation, faxes, letters, or interviews that cannot be accessed by other investigators. Therefore, in-text citations for personal communications—like the ones for Coetzee, Grossberg, and the anonymous US soldier—should fully describe the item, including the full date. Do not cite interviews conducted with research participants, since those are confidential.
Television program	Reference list	Benioff, D., & Weiss, D. B. (Writers), & Graves, A. (Director). (2014). The children [Television series episode]. In D. Benioff & D. Weiss (Executive Producers) *Game of Thrones*. New York, NY: HBO. Carlock, R. (Writer), & Miller, M. B. (Director). (2009). Into the crevasse [Television series episode]. In T. Fey, L. Michaels, M. Klein, D. Miner, & R. Carlock (Producers), *30 Rock*. NBC. Retrieved from http://www.hulu.com/30-rock
	In-text	(Benioff, Weiss, & Graves, 2014) (Carlock & Miller, 2009)
Film	Reference list	Wallis, H. B. (Producer), & Huston, J. (Director/Writer). (1941). *The Maltese falcon* [Motion picture]. H. Bogart, M. Astor, P. Lorre, S. Greenstreet, E. Cook Jr. (Performers). Based on novel by D. Hammett. Warner Studios. United States: Warner Home Video, DVD. (2000) Goolsby, K., & York, A. (Directors). (2015). *Tig* [Motion picture]. United States: Beachside Films and Netflix. Retrieved from www.netflix.com ▸ Required: You must include the title, director, studio, and year released.

    ▸ Optional: the actors, producers, screen-
      writers, editors, cinematographers, and other
      information. Include what you need for anal-
      ysis in your paper, in order of importance to
      your analysis. Their names appear between
      the title and the distributor.

    ▸ If a motion picture accessed online is behind
      a paywall or easily available by searching a
      site (such as Netflix or Hulu), just provide the
      home page URL.

	In-text	(Wallis & Huston, 1941/2000) (Goolsby & York, 2015)
Photograph	Reference list	Adams, A. (1927). *Monolith, the face of Half Dome, Yosemite National Park* [Photograph]. Art Institute, Chicago. Adams, A. (1927). *Monolith, the face of Half Dome, Yosemite National Park* [Photograph]. Art Institute, Chicago. Retrieved from http://www.hctc.commnet.edu/ artmuseum/anseladams/details/pdf/ monlith.pdf
	In-text	(Adams, 1927)
Figures: map, chart, graph, or table	Credit or explanation for figure or table	▸ Citation for a map, chart, graph, or table normally appears as a credit below the item rather than as an in-text citation. *Note.* 2016 House election results map. *Politico.* Retrieved from http://www.politico .com/mapdata-2016/2016-election/results/ map/house/ *Note.* From M. E. J. Newman (n.d.), Maps of the 2016 US presidential election. Retrieved from http://www-personal.umich.edu/ ~mejn/election/2016// *Note.* K. Smith, Urban Institute, (2013), Distribution of family income [Graph], 1963–2013. Retrieved from http://apps.urban.org/ features/wealth-inequality-charts/

Figures: map, chart, graph, or table (*continued*)		*Note.* From K. Menkhaus (2006/2007), Governance without government in Somalia: Spoilers, state building, and the politics of coping. *International Security*, *31* (Winter), 79, fig. 1. ▸ Give a descriptive title to your maps, charts, graphs, and tables. With this description, the reader should understand the item without having to refer to the text. *Note.* All figures are rounded to nearest percentile. ▸ This is a general note explaining information in a table. *p <.05 **p < .01. Both are two-tailed tests. ▸ This is a probability note for a table of statistics.
	Reference list	House election results map. (2016). *Politico.* Retrieved from http://www.politico.com/ mapdata-2016/2016-election/results/ map/house/ Newman, M. E. J. (n.d.). Maps of the 2016 US presidential election. Retrieved from http://www-personal.umich.edu/~mejn/ election/2016 K. Smith, Urban Institute. (2013). Distribution of family income [Graph]. 1963–2013. Retrieved from http://apps.urban .org/features/wealth-inequality-charts Menkhaus, K. (2006/2007). Governance without government in Somalia: Spoilers, state building, and the politics of coping. *International Security*, *31* (Winter), 74–106. https://doi.org/10.1162/isec.2007.31 .3.74
	In-text	(2016 House election results, 2016) (Newman, n.d.) (K. Smith, 2013) (Menkhaus, 2006/2007)
Musical recording	Reference list	Johnson, R. (1998). Last fair deal gone down. On *Robert Johnson: King of the Delta blues singers* (Exp. ed.) [CD]. Columbia/ Legacy. (Originally recorded 1936)

▸ "Exp. ed." = expanded edition.

Beyoncé. (2016). Formation. On *Lemonade*. Columbia / Parkwood Entertainment. Retrieved from http://tidal.com/us

In-text	(Johnson, 1936/1998, track 5) (Beyoncé, 2016, track 11)

Advertisement	Reference list	Advertisement for *Letters from Iwo Jima* [Motion picture]. (2007, February 6). *New York Times*, p. B4. Drink outside the Lines. (2017, June 15). [Advertisement for Vitamin Water]. *Rolling Stone*, 17. Tab cola. [ca. late 1960s]. Be a mindsticker [Television advertisement]. Retrieved from http://www.dailymotion.com/video/ ×2s3qi_1960s-tab-commercial-be-a-mind stick_ads ▸ Enclose estimated dates in square brackets.
	In-text	(advertisement for *Letters from Iwo Jima*, 2007) (Vitamin Water, 2017) (Tab cola [ca. late 1960s])

Government document	Reference list	*A bill to promote the national security by providing for a national defense establishment: Hearings on S. 758 before the Committee on Armed Service, Senate*, 80th Cong. 1 (1947). ▸ "80th Cong. 1" refers to page 1 (not to the first session). If the reference was to testimony by a specific individual, that would appear after the date: (1947) (testimony of Gen. George Marshall). ▸ For documents printed by the Government Printing Office, give the full name rather than the initials GPO. National Institute on Aging. (2015). *Caring for a person with Alzheimer's disease: Your easy-to-use guide from the National Institute on Aging*. Washington, DC: US Government Printing Office. ▸ or

Government document (*continued*)		National Institute on Aging. (2015). *Caring for a person with Alzheimer's disease: Your easy-to-use guide from the National Institute on Aging*. Retrieved from https://permanent.access.gpo.gov/gpo66296/caring-for-a-person-with-alzheimers-disease.pdf Public Safety Canada (2017, September 24). Minister Goodale pays tribute to fallen police and peace officers. Retrieved from https://www.canada.ca/en/public-safety-canada/news/2017/09/minister_goodalepaystributetofallenpoliceand peaceofficers.html Federal Bureau of Investigation [FBI]. (1972). *Investigation of John Lennon* (248 pages). Retrieved from http:// foia.fbi.gov/foia index/lennon.htm
	In-text	(*Bill to promote national security*, 1947) (National Institute on Aging, 2015) (Public Safety Canada, 2017) (FBI, 1972)
Database or data set	Reference list	Maryland Department of Assessments and Taxation. (2017). *Real property data search*. Retrieved from https://sdat.dat.maryland.gov/RealProperty/Pages/default.aspx US Copyright Office. (2017). *Search copyright records*. Retrieved from http://www.copy right.gov/records/ Gleditsch, K. S., & Chiozza, G. (2009). *Archigos: A data base on leaders, 1875–2004* (Version 2.9). Retrieved from http://mail.rochester.edu/%7Ehgoemans/data.htm Pew Research Center. (2014). *Religious landscape study*. Retrieved from http://www.pewforum.org/religious-landscape-study/ United Nations Treaty Collection. (2010). *Databases*. Retrieved from http://treaties.un.org/ ▶ For a specific item within this database:

Convention on the prevention and punishment of the crime of genocide. (1948). In
United Nations Treaty Collection, *Databases*. Retrieved from https://treaties
.un.org/doc/Treaties/1951/01/19510112
%2008-12%20PM/Ch_IV_1p.pdf

In-text	(Maryland Department of Assessments, 2017) (US Copyright Office, 2017) (Gleditsch & Chiozza, 2009) (United Nations Treaty Collection, 2010) (Convention on the prevention and punish-ment of the crime of genocide, 1948)

Diagnostic test	Reference list	*MMPI-2: Restructured clinical (RC) scales.* (2003). Minneapolis: University of Minnesota Press. Ben-Porath, Y. S., & Tellegen, A. (2008). *MMPI-2-RF (Minnesota Multiphasic Personality Inventory-2): Manual for administration, scoring, and interpretation.* Minneapolis: University of Minnesota Press. ▸ Manual for administering the test. Ben-Porath, Y. S. (2012). *Interpreting the MMPI-2-RF.* Minneapolis: University of Minnesota Press. ▸ Interpretive manual for the test. Q Local (Version 3.3) [Computer software]. (2017). Minneapolis, MN: Pearson Assessments. ▸ Scoring software for the test.
	In-text	(*MMPI-2 RC scales*, 2003) (Ben-Porath & Tellegen, 2008) (Ben-Porath, 2012) (Q Local, 2017)

Diagnostic manual	Reference list	Lingiardi, V., & McWilliams, M. (Eds.). (2017). *Psychodynamic diagnostic manual* (2nd ed.). New York, NY: Guilford Press. American Psychiatric Association. (2000). *Diagnostic and statistical manual of mental disorders* (4th ed., text rev. [*DSM-IV-TR*]). Washington, DC: Author.

Diagnostic manual (*continued*)		▶ or American Psychiatric Association. (2000). *Diagnostic and statistical manual of mental disorders* (4th ed., text rev. [*DSM-IV-TR*]). https://doi.org/10.1176/appi.books.9780890423349
	In-text	(Lingiardi & McWilliams, 2017) (American Psychiatric Association, *Diagnostic and statistical manual of mental disorders* [*DSM-IV-TR*], 2000) for the first use only. (*DSM-IV-TR*) for second use and later. Title is italicized.
Website, page or entire	Reference list	American Historical Association [Home page]. (2017). Retrieved August 1, 2017, from https://www.historians.org ▶ Many webpages do not have identifiable authors. List the organization that sponsors the website instead. Lipson, C. (2010). "Advice on getting a good recommendation." Retrieved from http://www.charleslipson.com/Getting-a-good-recommendation.htm *The Dick Van Dyke show*: Series summary. (n.d.). *Sitcoms online*. Retrieved from http://www.sitcomsonline.com/thedickvandykeshow.html ▶ If a website or webpage does not show a date when it was copyrighted or updated, then list (n.d.) where the year normally appears. ▶ It is usually sufficient to provide the address of the website in the text.
	In-text	(American Historical Association, 2017) (Lipson, 2010) (*The Dick Van Dyke show*: Series summary, n.d.)
Blog, post or comment	Reference list	Pearce, F. (2017, September 18). In a stunning turnaround, Britain moves to end the burning of coal. [Blog post]. *Yale Environment 360*. Retrieved from http://e360.yale.edu/features/in-a-stunning-turnaround-britain-moves-to-end-the-burning-of-coal

▸ If this post had no title, it would be cited thus:

Pearce, F. (2017, September 18). Untitled. [Blog post. *Yale Environment 360* . . .

Dinah. (2017, August 1). Inpatient psychiatry: Not all bad. [Blog post]. *Shrink Rap*. Retrieved from http://psychiatrist-blog .blogspot.com/

Catlover. (2017, August 5). Re: Inpatient psychiatry: Not all bad. [Blog comment]. *Shrink Rap*. Retrieved from https:// www.blogger.com/comment.g?blogID =26666124&postID=4980105132352 25858

▸ If "Catlover" had commented several times the same day and there was no link to a specific comment, then you should include the time: (2017, August 5, 12:53 a.m.).

In-text

(Pearce, 2017)
(Dinah, 2017)
(Catlover, 2017)

Video   Reference list   Archer Productions (Producer). (1951). *Duck and cover* [Video file]. Produced for the Federal Civil Defense Administration. Retrieved from https://en.wikipedia.org/ wiki/File:DuckandC1951.ogv

Jury convicts Martin Shkreli on three counts of security fraud. (2017, August 4). [Video file]. Retrieved from https://www .nbcnews.com/video/jury-convicts-martin -shkreli-on-three-counts-of-securities -fraud-1017719875664

Wang, T. (2016, September). The human insights missing from big data. [Video file]. Retrieved from https://www.ted .com/talks/tricia_wang_the_human _insights_missing_from_big_data

Stevens, M. (2017, July 17). How much of the earth can you see at once? [Video file]. Retrieved from https://youtu.be/ mxhxL1LzKww

Windfall. (July 29, 2017).

Video *(continued)*		Re: How much of the earth can you see at once? [Comment on video blog post]. Retrieved from https://youtu.be/mxhxL1 LzKww ▸ When the URL is very long and the video can be found on a searchable site, you may choose to include only the site's main page: Retrieved from https://www.ted.com/
	In-text	(Archer Productions, 1951) ("Jury convicts Martin Shkreli," 2017) (Wang, 2016) (Stevens, 2017) (Windfall, 2017)
Multimedia app and software	Reference list	▸ APA cites apps (mobile application software) and computer software the same way. ▸ You do not need to include standard software, like Microsoft or Adobe, in the reference list, but do include specialty software and apps. EA Sports. (2017). Madden NFL 18 [Video game]. Retrieved from https://www .easports.com/madden-nfl Groundspeak. (2017). Geocaching. (v. 5.6.1) [Mobile application software]. Retrieved from https://www.geocaching.com/play Mathworks. (2014). Matlab. (versionR2014b) [Computer software]. Retrieved from https://www.mathworks.com/products/ matlab.html
	In-text	(EA Sports, 2017) (Groundspeak, 2017) (Mathworks, 2014) (Microsoft home & business, 2016)
Podcast	Reference list	Burriss, R. (Producer). (2017, August 1). Conflict and reconciliation [Audio podcast]. In *The Psychology of Attractiveness*. Retrieved from http://psychologyofattractivenesspodcast.blogspot.com/2017/08/ conflict-and-reconciliation-01-aug-2017 .html ▸ Or to avoid the long URL:

Burriss, R. (Producer). (2017, August 1). Conflict and reconciliation [Audio podcast]. In *The Psychology of Attractiveness.* Retrieved from http://psychologyof attractivenesspodcast.blogspot.com

Shipping container grow rooms, Uber for dogs, and plutonium on Pluto. (2015, July 27). [Video podcast]. In *Geekbeat.* Retrieved from http://geekbeat.tv/ shipping-container-grow-rooms-uber-for -dogs-and-plutonium-on-pluto/

▶ or

Draney, G. (Host). (2015, July 27). Shipping container grow rooms, Uber for dogs, and plutonium on Pluto. [Video podcast]. In *Geekbeat.* Retrieved from http://geek beat.tv

In-text	(Burris, 2017) "Shipping container," 2015) ▶ or (Draney, 2015)

Social media (Facebook, Instagram, Twitter)	Reference list	Simpson, M. [Maggie]. (n.d.) [Profile]. Retrieved from http://www.facebook .com/maggiesimpson ▶ When initials are not enough (in this case, let's pretend Maggie happened to be listed as an author in the references also), add a first name in square brackets. In text, cite the full name. Grammar Girl. (2017, October 5). Diminutives often express smallness [Facebook status update]. Retrieved from https:// www.facebook.com/GrammarGirl/posts/ 10157671243605228 Tyson, N. D. [neiltyson]. (2017, July 7, 1:25pm). Always seemed to me that millipedes have more legs than are necessary [Tweet]. Retrieved from https://twitter.com/neiltyson/status/ 883421859072458752

Social media (Facebook, Instagram, Twitter) (*continued*)		► Provide the address ("permalink") for the archived version of the message or page if possible. On sites like Facebook and Twitter, the archived message URL can be accessed via the date and time stamp. Richards, C. [coryrichards]. (2017, May 4). A quiet if not solemn day on Everest [Instagram photo]. Retrieved from https://www.instagram.com/p/BUekBZLgDOW/
	In-text	(Maggie Simpson, n.d.) (Grammar Girl, 2017) (Tyson, 2017) (Richards, 2017)
Email, texts (direct messages)	Reference list	► Personal emails, texts, and other instant messages are not included in the reference list because they cannot be retrieved by third parties. You should include items that can be accessed through a URL. Abrams, J. (2015, April 28). Fw: a Favor. [Email]. Retrieved from https://assets.documentcloud.org/documents/3516674/Abrams-amp-Bank-Phoenix-Electric.pdf
	In-text	(Abrams, 2015) ► Because personal emails and instant messages are not included in the reference list, they should be fully described in the text. (E. Leis, email message to author, 2018, May 3) (M. H. Lipson, instant message to J. S. Lipson, 2015, March 9) ► You may include the time of an electronic message if it is important or differentiates it from others. For example: (M. H. Lipson, instant message to J. S. Lipson, 2015, March 9, 11:23 a.m.)
Electronic forum or mailing list	Reference list	► Nonarchived messages to mailing lists or discussion groups are also not included in the reference list because they cannot be retrieved by third parties. You should include items that can be accessed through a URL.

Ngo, Q. (2017, July 14). Re: what are some unknown truths about college life? [Online forum comment]. Retrieved from https://www.quora.com/What-are-some -unknown-truths-about-college-life

▸ Include the user's real name, if known, with screen name in brackets. The screen name is sufficient if the real name is unknown.

▸ If the name of the group or list is not evident from the URL, you must include it in the reference.

In-text   (Ngo, 2017)

APA does not permit very many abbreviations in its reference lists. When it does, it sometimes wants them capitalized and sometimes not. Who knows why?

APA: COMMON ABBREVIATIONS IN REFERENCE LISTS

chapter	chap.	part	Pt.
edition	ed.	revised edition	Rev. ed.
editor	Ed.	second edition	2nd ed.
no date	n.d.	supplement	Suppl.
number	No.	translated by	Trans.
page	p.	volume	Vol. (e.g., Vols. 2–5)
pages	pp.	volumes	vols. (e.g., 3 vols.)

6 CSE CITATIONS FOR THE BIOLOGICAL SCIENCES

CSE citations, devised by the Council of Science Editors, are widely used for scientific papers, journals, and books in the life sciences. The citations are based on international principles adopted by the National Library of Medicine. Detailed information about CSE citations for the sciences can be found in *Scientific Style and Format: The CSE Manual for Authors, Editors, and Publishers*, 8th ed. (Chicago: University of Chicago Press, 2014), which is also available online at www.scientificstyleandformat.org.

Actually the CSE system lets you choose among three ways of citing documents:

- *Citation-sequence*: Citations are numbered (1), (2), (3), in the order they appear in the text. Full references appear at the end of the paper—in the same order. They are *not* alphabetized.
- *Citation-name*: Citations are numbered, with full references at the end of the paper, in alphabetical order. The first item cited in the text might be number 8 on the alphabetical list. It would be cited as (8), even though it appeared first—and (8) if it appears again.
- *Name-year*: Citations in the text are given as name and year, such as (McClintock 2017). Full references appear at the end of the paper in alphabetical order, just as they do in APA citations.

Whichever format you choose, use it consistently throughout the paper. Ask your instructor which one she prefers.

Citation-sequence. Cite the first reference in the text as number 1, the second as number 2, and so on. You can use brackets [1], superscripts[1], or parentheses (1). At the end of the paper, list all the items, beginning with the first one cited. The list is *not* alphabetical. If the first item you cite is by Professor Zangwill, then that's the first item in the reference list. If you cite Zangwill's paper again, it's still [1], even if it's the last citation in your paper. If you want to cite several items at once, simply include the number for each one, separated by commas, such as [1,3,9] or [1,3,9] or (1,3,9). If items have successive numbers, use hyphens: 4–6,12–18.

Citation-name. Begin by assembling an alphabetical list of references at the end of the text and numbering them. Each item in the list will have a number, which is used whenever that book or article is cited in the text. If the Zangwill article is thirty-sixth in the alphabetical list, then it is always cited with that number, even if it's the first item you cite in the paper. The next reference in the text might be [23], the one after that might be [12]. Citations can be set as superscripts, in brackets, or in parentheses. If you want to cite several items at once, include a number for each one, such as [4,15,22] or [4,15,22] or (4,15,22). Use hyphens for continuous numbers (1–3). So a citation of multiple sources could be (4,16–18,22).

Name-year. For in-text citations, use the (name-year) format without commas, such as (Cronin and Siegler 2016) and (Siegler et al. 2017). The reference list is alphabetical by author and includes all cited articles. If an author has several articles, list the earliest ones first. Follow the same method if an author has published several articles in the same year. List the first one as 2017a, the second as 2017b, and so on by the month of publication. To cite several articles by Susan Lindquist, then, the notation might be (Lindquist 2014d, 2013a, 2017h), referring to those three articles in the reference list.

In the same way, you can also cite articles by different authors within the same reference. Separate them with semicolons, such as (Liebman 2017; Ma and Lindquist 2013; Outeiro and Lindquist 2015).

If the author's name appears in the sentence, you do not need to repeat it in the citation. For example, "According to LaBarbera (2010), this experiment . . ."

What if LaBarbera had ten or fifteen coauthors? That's certainly possible in the sciences. Articles sometimes have dozens of authors because they include everyone involved in the experiments leading to publication. My colleague Henry Frisch, a high-energy physicist, told me that one of his articles has nearly eight hundred coauthors![1] I grew up in a town with a phone book shorter than that. Really.

How many of these authors should you include when you use name-year

---

1. Professor Frisch's own practice is to list himself as author only if he actually helped write the paper. His practice is unusual, but a number of scientists think that he's right—that current practices are unclear and often lax. To correct the problem, some scientists are circulating proposals that would require coauthors to specify how they contributed to joint papers. For Frisch's comments on the metastasizing growth of coauthors, see his webpage, http://hep.uchicago.edu/~frisch/authorship.pdf.

citations in the text? Don't go overboard. Just list the first seven hundred. If you do that in the first sentence, you'll reach the paper's word limit before you even have to write a second sentence. That's one easy science paper.

Actually, CSE offers clear recommendations, stopping a bit short of seven hundred authors. If there are only two authors, list them both, separated by "and." If there are three or more authors, list only the first one, followed by "et al." For example: (LaBarbera et al. 2010). Later I'll show you how to handle coauthors in the reference list at the end of the paper.

QUICK COMPARISON OF CSE STYLES

Style	In-text citations	Reference list at end of paper
Citation-sequence	(1), (2), (3), (4)	Items listed in order of their text appearance
Citation-name	(31), (2), (13), (7)	Items listed alphabetically, by author surname
Name-year	(Shapiro 2016)	Items listed alphabetically, by author surname

STYLES OF REFERENCE LISTS

All three styles require reference lists following the text. CSE emphasizes brevity and simplicity for these lists. Instead of using the authors' first names, use only their initials. Omit periods after the initials and don't put spaces between them: Stern HK.

Shorten journal names with standard abbreviations, such as those listed in the PubMed journals database available at http://www.ncbi.nlm.nih.gov/journals. CSE doesn't use periods in shortening journal titles. So J Biosci Bioeng (without periods) is the abbreviation for the *Journal of Bioscience and Bioengineering*.

CSE uses sentence-style capitalization for titles. Capitalize only the first word, proper nouns, and the first word after a colon. Format the titles in normal type rather than italics.

If you cite something you've read online rather than in print, cite the electronic version. After all, the two versions may differ. To do that, CSE style requires you to add a couple of items to the citation: (1) the dates the document was modified or posted and the date you accessed it and (2) the URL and/or DOI. A URL based on a DOI (appended to https://doi.org/) is preferable to another kind of URL.

Print citation	Pantazopoulou M, Boban M, Foisner R, Ljungdahl PO. 2016. Cdc48 and Ubx1 participate in a pathway associated with the inner nuclear membrane that governs Asi1 degradation. J Cell Sci. 129(20):3770–3780.
Online citation	Pantazopoulou M, Boban M, Foisner R, Ljungdahl PO. 2016. Cdc48 and Ubx1 participate in a pathway associated with the inner nuclear membrane that governs Asi1 degradation. J Cell Sci. [accessed 2017 Sep 14];129(20):3770–3780. https://doi.org/10.1242/jcs.189332.

This article, like nearly all printed articles, was not modified after it was published. But preprints are often modified, and so are articles in electronic journals. You need to include that information in the citation so your readers will know which version you are citing. That information appears in the square brackets, immediately before the date you accessed the item.

Modified paper	Pantazopoulou M, Boban M, Foisner R, Ljungdahl PO. 2016. Cdc48 and Ubx1 participate in a pathway associated with the inner nuclear membrane that governs Asi1 degradation. J Cell Sci. [modified 2016 Dec 2; accessed 2017 Sep 14];129(20):3770–3780. https://doi.org/10.1242/jcs.189332.

Don't worry about remembering all these details. There are too many of them. I'll explain them in the tables that follow and include plenty of examples. If you use this style often, you'll gradually grow familiar with the fine points.

These tables show CSE recommendations for in-text citations and reference lists, using all three formats. Not every journal follows them exactly, so you'll see some variation as you read scientific publications. Journals differ, for example, in how many coauthors they include in the reference list. Some list only the first three authors before adding "et al." One lists the first twenty-six. (Imagine being poor coauthor number 27.) The CSE says to name up to ten and then add "et al."

CSE: NAME-YEAR SYSTEM

Journal article	Reference list	Dannemann M, Kelso J. 2017. The contribution of Neanderthals to phenotypic variation in modern humans. Am J Hum Genet. 101(4):578–589.

► CSE does not require the issue number for consecutively paginated journal volumes like this one, but it's always okay to include it.

Wong KK et al. 2007. A comprehensive analysis of common copy-number variations in the human genome. Am J Hum Genet. 80(1):91–104.

► The Wong article has eleven authors. CSE says to list the first ten, followed by "et al." But individual journals vary in their practice. Some would include all of them in the reference list. Most would include only the first two.

Guerrero-Sanchez VM et al. 2017. Holm oak (*Queras ilex*) transcriptome. *De novo* sequencing and assembly analysis. Front Mol Biosci [modified 2017 Oct 6; accessed 2017 Oct 21];4:70. https://doi.org/10 .3389/fmolb.2017.00070.

► Note the unusual way that dates are written in this CSE style: 2017 Oct 21.

In-text   (Dannemann and Kelso 2017)
(Wong et al. 2007)

► If your list includes several publications by Wong and other authors in 2007, your in-text reference should include coauthors to clarify exactly which article you are citing. For example: (Wong, deLeeuw, et al. 2007).

(Guerrero-Sanchez et al. 2017)

Book, one author	Reference list	Bickley LS. 2016. Bates' guide to physical examination and history taking. Alphen aan de Rijn (Netherlands): Wolters Kluwer.

Vetter RS. 2015. The brown recluse spider. Ithaca (NY): Cornell University Press.

► If the publisher's city is well known, you may omit the state.

	In-text	(Bickley 2016) (Vetter 2015) ▶ To cite the same author for works written in several years: (Vetter 2015, 2016a, 2016b, 2018) ▶ To cite works by authors with the same surname published in the same year, include the authors' initials: (Vetter RS 2015;Vetter T 2015)
Book, multiple authors	Reference list	Provost JJ, Colabroy KL, Kelly BS, Wallert MA. 2016. The science of cooking: Understanding the biology and chemistry behind food and cooking. Hoboken (NJ): John Wiley & Sons. ▶ In the reference list, name up to ten authors, then add "et al."
	In-text	(Provost et al. 2016) ▶ If there are just two authors, name them both: (Provost and Colabroy 2016)
Book, online or e-book	Reference list	Schmitz OJ. 2016. The new ecology: Rethinking a science for the Anthropocene. Princeton (NJ): Princeton University Press. [accessed 2017 Oct 22]. Google Play Books. ▶ Include a URL or DOI at the end of the reference, instead of device or service, if the book is read online.
	In-text	(Schmitz 2016)
Book, multiple editions	Reference list	Gerard JE. 2014. Principles of environmental chemistry. 3rd ed. Burlington (MA): Jones and Bartlett. Snell RS. 2007. Clinical anatomy by regions. 8th ed. Philadelphia: Lippincott Williams & Wilkins. ▶ For a revised edition, use the phrase "Rev. ed." instead of "8th ed."
	In-text	(Gerard 2014) (Snell 2007)

Book, multiple editions, no author	Reference list	Publication manual of the American Psychological Association. 2010. 6th ed. Washington (DC): American Psychological Association.
	In-text	(Publication manual . . . 2010) ▶ Do not use "Anonymous" in place of the author name. Instead, use the first word or first few words of the title and an ellipsis, followed by the date.
Book, edited	Reference list	Rish, I, Cecchi GA, Lozano A, Niculescu-Mizil A, editors. 2014. Practical applications of sparse modeling. Cambridge (MA): MIT Press.
	In-text	(Rish et al. 2014)
Chapter in edited book	Reference list	McGrath J. 2015. Environmental factors and gene-environment interactions. In: Mitchell KJ, editor. The genetics of neurodevelopmental disorders. Hoboken (NJ): John Wiley and Sons. p. 111–127.
	In-text	(McGrath 2015)
Preprint	Reference list	Muir CD. 2017. Light and growth form interact to shape stomatal ratio among British angiosperms. Preprint. bioRxiv. [posted 2017 Jul 14, accessed 2017 Oct 22]. https://doi.org/10.1101/163873. ▶ CSE's 8th edition of *Style and Format* does not specify a style for citing preprints. The format shown here is consistent, however, with other citation rules in that edition.
	In-text	(Muir 2017)
Government document, hard copy or online	Reference list	Marinopoulos SS, Dorman T, Ratanawongsa N, Wilson LM, Ashar BH, Magaziner JL, Miller RG, Thomas PA, Prokopowicz GP, Qayyum R, et al. 2007. Effectiveness of continuing medical education. Rockville (MD): Agency for Healthcare Research and Quality. AHRQ Pub. No. 07-E006.

[EPA] Environmental Protection Agency (US), Office of Air and Radiation, Indoor Environments Division. 2012. A brief guide to mold, moisture, and your home. Washington (DC): EPA. [modified 2012 Sep 1; accessed 2015 Nov 28]. https://www.epa .gov/nscep.

▶ If an organization is both author and publisher, the name may be abbreviated as publisher.

In-text	(Marinopoulos et al. 2007) (EPA 2012)

Video	Reference list	3D human anatomy: Regional edition [DVD-ROM]. 2009. London (England): Primal Pictures.
		The secret social life of a solitary puma [video]. 2017 Oct 12, 1:43 minutes. Scientific American. [accessed 2017 Nov 19]. https://www.scientificamerican.com/ video/the-secret-social-live-of-a-solitary -puma/.
	In-text	(3D human anatomy 2009) (Secret social life 2017)

Database	Reference list	RCSB Protein Data Bank. 1971– . [accessed 2017 Aug 1]. http://www.rcsb.org/pdb/ home/home.do.
		Swedish Life Sciences Database. [date unknown]– . Zurich (Switzerland): Venture Valuation. [accessed 2017 Sep 15]. http:// www.swedishlifesciences.com/se/portal/ index.php.

▶ Both databases are continually updated. List the year they began or "[date unknown]," followed by an en dash or hyphen and a space.

In-text	(RCSB Protein Data Bank 1971–) (Swedish Life Sciences Database [accessed 2017])

▶ Use the access date if no other date is listed.

Website, webpage, or blog	Reference list	[CSE] Council of Science Editors. c2017. Wheat Ridge (CO): Council of Science Editors; [accessed 2017 Oct 19]. https://www.councilscienceeditors.org/resource-library/editorial-policies/cse-policies/. ▶ Include the date of publication or the date copyrighted (c2017) if available. [USDA] US Department of Agriculture, Agricultural Research Service. Washington (DC): USDA; [modified 2017 Feb 2; accessed 2017 Nov 8]. https://www.ars.usda.gov/. Haran M. 2016 Sep 7. Active parenting behaviors of the Caribbean spiny lobster. BMC series blog. [accessed 2017 Jul 29]. https://blogs.biomedcentral.com/bmcseriesblog/2016/09/07/active-parenting-behaviors-caribbean-spiny-lobster. ▶ If it is not obvious that the article is from a blog, insert [blog] after the date.
	In-text	(CSE c2017) (USDA 2017) (Haran 2016)
Podcast	Reference list	Semple, I. Tomorrow's technology: From asteroid mining to programmable matter. 2017 Nov 15, 30:42 minutes. The Guardian science weekly podcast. [accessed 2017 Nov 19]. https://www.theguardian.com/science/audio/2017/nov/15/tomorrows-technology-from-asteroid-mining-to-programmable-matter-science-weekly-podcast.
	In-text	(Semple 2017)

The next table shows CSE references using citation-sequence and citation-name formats. The main difference from the previous table is that the date appears later in the reference. I have used the same examples, in case you want to compare formats.

CSE: CITATION-SEQUENCE AND CITATION-NAME SYSTEMS

Journal article	Reference list	Dannemann M, Kelso J. The contribution of Neanderthals to phenotypic variation in modern humans. Am J Hum Genet. 2017;101(4):578–589.
		Wong KK, deLeeuw RJ, et al. A comprehensive analysis of common copy-number variations in the human genome. Am J Hum Genet. 2007;80(1):91–104.
		Guerrero-Sanchez VM, et al. Holm oak (*Queras ilex*) transcriptome. *De novo* sequencing and assembly analysis. Front Mol Biosci. 2017 [modified 2017 Oct 6; accessed 2017 Oct 21];4:70. https://doi .org/10.3389/fmolb.2017.00070.
Book, one author	Reference list	Bickley LS. Bates' guide to physical examination and history taking. Alphen aan de Rijn (Netherlands): Wolters Kluwer; 2016.
		Vetter RS. The brown recluse spider. Ithaca (NY): Cornell University Press; 2015.
Book, multiple authors	Reference list	Provost JJ, Colabroy KL, Kelly BS, Wallert MA. The science of cooking: Understanding the biology and chemistry behind food and cooking. Hoboken (NJ): John Wiley & Sons; 2016.
		▸ In the reference list, name up to ten authors, then add "et al."
Book, online or e-book	Reference list	Schmitz OJ. The new ecology: rethinking a science for the Anthropocene. Princeton (NJ): Princeton University Press; 2016 [accessed 2017 Oct 22]. Google Play Books.
		▸ Include a URL or DOI at the end of the reference if the book is read online.
Book, multiple editions	Reference list	Gerard JE. Principles of environmental chemistry. 3rd ed. Burlington (MA): Jones and Bartlett; 2014. Snell RS. Clinical anatomy by regions. 8th ed. Philadelphia: Lippincott Williams & Wilkins; 2007.

Book, multiple editions, no author	Reference list	Publication manual of the American Psychological Association. 6th ed. Washington (DC): American Psychological Association; 2010.
Book, edited	Reference list	Rish, I, Cecchi GA, Lozano A, Niculescu-Mizil A, editors. Practical applications of sparse modeling. Cambridge (MA): MIT Press; 2014.
Chapter in edited book	Reference list	McGrath J. Environmental factors and gene-environment interactions. In: Mitchell KJ, editor. The genetics of neurodevelopmental disorders. Hoboken (NJ): John Wiley and Sons; 2015. p. 111–127.
Preprint	Reference list	Muir CD. Light and growth form interact to shape stomatal ratio among British angiosperms. Preprint. bioRxiv; 2017 [posted 2017 Jul 14, accessed 2017 Oct 22]. https://doi.org/10.1101/163873.
Government document	Reference list	Marinopoulos SS, Dorman T, Ratanawongsa N, Wilson LM, Ashar BH, Magaziner JL, Miller RG, Thomas PA, Prokopowicz GP, Qayyum R, Bass EB. Effectiveness of continuing medical education. Rockville (MD): Agency for Healthcare Research and Quality; 2007. AHRQ Pub. No. 07-E006.
		[EPA] Environmental Protection Agency (US), Office of Air and Radiation, Indoor Environments Division. A brief guide to mold, moisture, and your home. Washington (DC): EPA; 2012 [modified 2012 Sep 1; accessed 2015 Nov 28]. https://www.epa.gov/nscep.
Video	Reference list	3D human anatomy: Regional edition [DVD-ROM]. London (England): Primal Pictures; 2009.

The secret social life of a solitary puma [video]. Scientific American. 2017 Oct 12, 1:43. [accessed 2017 Nov 19]. https://www .scientificamerican.com/video/the-secret -social-live-of-a-solitary-puma.

Database	Reference list	RCSB Protein Data Bank. 1971– [accessed 2017 Aug 1]. http://www.rcsb.org/pdb/ home/home.do
		Swedish Life Sciences Database. Zurich (Switzerland): Venture Valuation. [date unknown]– [accessed 2017 Sep 15]. http:// www.swedishlifesciences.com/se/portal/ index.php.
Website, web- page, or blog	Reference list	[CSE] Council of Science Editors. Wheat Ridge (CO): Council of Science Editors; c2017 [accessed 2017 Oct 19]. https:// www.councilscienceeditors.org/resource -library/editorial-policies/cse-policies/.
		[USDA] US Department of Agriculture, Agricultural Research Service. Washing- ton (DC): USDA; [modified 2017 Feb 2; accessed 2017 Nov 8]. https://www.ars .usda.gov/.
		Haran M. Active parenting behaviors of the Caribbean spiny lobster. BMC series blog. 2016 Sep 7 [accessed 2017 Jul 29]. https://blogs.biomedcentral.com/ bmcseriesblog/2016/09/07/active -parenting-behaviors-caribbean-spiny -lobster.
Podcast	Reference list	Semple I. Tomorrow's technology: From asteroid mining to programmable matter. The Guardian science weekly podcast. 2017 Nov 15, 30:42 minutes [accessed 2017 Nov 19]. https://www.theguardian .com/science/audio/2017/nov/15/ tomorrows-technology-from-asteroid -mining-to-programmable-matter-science -weekly-podcast.

Although individual references (shown above) are the same for both the citation-sequence and citation-name systems, their full reference lists are compiled in different orders.

Order of items within reference lists:

- Citation-name system: alphabetical by author
- Citation-sequence system: order of first appearance in the text

To illustrate, let's take the opening sentence of an article and show how each style would handle the citations and reference list.

CSE: CITATION-SEQUENCE SYSTEM
(ILLUSTRATION OF REFERENCE LIST ORDER)

Opening sentence	This research deals with the ABC transporter family and builds on prior studies by Nguyen et al.,[1] Sheps et al.,[2] and Kerr.[3]
Reference list (in order of appearance in text)	1. Nguyen VNT, Moon S, Jung, K. Molecular biology: Genome-wide expression analysis of rice ABC transporter family across spatio-temporal samples and in response to abiotic stresses. J Plant Physiol. 2014;171(14):1276–1288. 2. Sheps JA, Ralph S, Zhao Z, Baillie DL, Ling V. The ABC transporter gene family of Caenorhabditis elegans has implications for the evolutionary dynamics of multidrug resistance in eukaryotes. Genome Biol. 2004;5(3):R15. 3. Kerr ID. Sequence analysis of twin ATP binding cassette proteins involved in translational control, antibiotic resistance, and ribonuclease L inhibition. Biochem Biophys Res Commun. 2004;315(1):166–173. ▸ Nguyen's article is listed first because it is the first one mentioned in the text.

CSE: CITATION-NAME SYSTEM
(ILLUSTRATION OF REFERENCE LIST ORDER)

Opening sentence	This research deals with the ABC transporter family and builds on prior studies by Nguyen et al.,[2] Sheps et al.,[3] and Kerr.[1]
Reference list (alphabetical)	1. Kerr ID. Sequence analysis of twin ATP binding cassette proteins involved in translational control, antibiotic resistance, and ribonuclease L inhibition. Biochem Biophys Res Commun. 2004;315:166–173.

2. Nguyen VNT, Moon S, Jung, K. Molecular biology: Genome-wide expression analysis of rice ABC transporter family across spatio-temporal samples and in response to abiotic stresses. J Plant Physiol. 2014;171(14):1276–1288.
3. Sheps JA, Ralph S, Zhao Z, Baillie DL, Ling V. The ABC transporter gene family of Caenorhabditis elegans has implications for the evolutionary dynamics of multidrug resistance in eukaryotes. Genome Biol. 2004;5:R15.
► Nguyen's article is listed second because it is second alphabetically.

The two systems, citation-sequence and citation-name, present *each item* in the reference list the same way. What's different are (1) the *order* of items in the reference list and (2) their *citation numbers* in the text.

There's one more item you may wish to include in your citations: the PMID number. All medical articles have this electronic tag, which identifies them within the comprehensive PubMed database. The PMID appears as the last item in the citation and is *not* followed by a period:

Christakos S. In search of regulatory circuits that control the biological activity of vitamin D. J Biol Chem. 2017 Oct 20;292(42):17559–17560. PMID: 29055009

The PubMed database, covering more than four thousand biomedical journals, was developed at the National Library of Medicine and is available online at http://www.ncbi.nlm.nih.gov/pubmed/.

7 AMA CITATIONS FOR THE BIOMEDICAL SCIENCES, MEDICINE, NURSING, AND DENTISTRY

AMA citations are used in biomedical research, medicine, nursing, dentistry, and some related fields of biology. They are based on the *AMA Manual of Style: A Guide for Authors and Editors*, 10th ed. (Oxford: Oxford University Press, 2007), and the *AMA Manual of Style* online (www.ama manualofstyle.com), which is periodically updated.

Citations are numbered (1), (2), (3), in the order they appear in the text. Full references appear at the end of the paper—in the same order. For coauthored books and articles, you should list up to six authors. If there are more, list only the first three, followed by "et al." Rather than using the authors' first names, use their initials (without periods) and do not put spaces between the initials: Lipson CH. Abbreviate the titles of journals. Journal titles along with their standard abbreviations can be found in the PubMed journals database available at http://www.ncbi.nlm.nih .gov/journals.

AMA CITATIONS

Journal article   Neto AS, Schultz MJ. Optimizing the settings on the ventilator: high PEEP for all? *JAMA*. 2017;317(4):1413–1414.

> ▸ AMA uses sentence style for journal article titles and does *not* capitalize the first letter of a subtitle.

Drinka PJ, Krause PF, Nest LJ, Goodman BM. Determinants of vitamin D levels in nursing home residents. *J Am Med Dir Assoc*. 2007;8(2):76–79.

> ▸ Journal titles are abbreviated without periods. (There's a period after *Assoc.* only to separate the journal title from the information about date, volume and issue, and pagination.)

Ho EC, Parker JD, Austin PC, Tu JV, Wang X, Lee DS. Impact of nitrate use on survival in acute heart failure: a propensity-matched analysis. *Am Heart J*. 2016;5(2):e002531. https://doi.org/10.1161/JAHA.115.002531

Liu J, Xiong E, Zhu H, et al. Efficient induction of Ig gene hypermutation in ex-vivo-activated primary B cells. *J Immunol.* 2017;199(9)3023–3030. http://www.jimmunol .org/content/199/9/3023. Accessed October 5, 2017.

► Digital Object Identifiers (DOIs) are available for many journal articles—in fact, it's becoming hard to find an extant medical journal that doesn't assign them. A URL based on a DOI (appended to https://doi.org/) is preferable to another kind of URL. When you cite a DOI, you do not have to list a URL or an access date. An access date is required, however, if you list a URL.

► For citations of journal articles, AMA recommends copying the URL from the address bar in your browser rather than citing a home page—apparently without regard for length.

► Online journals do not always have page numbers. You may include other identifiers such as an article or e-page number if available.

► Name up to six authors in articles or books. If there are more, name the first three, then use "et al." This article, for example, has fifteen listed authors:

Watson LM, Bamber E, Schnekenberg, et al. Dominant muta-tions in GRM1 cause spinocerebellar. *Am J Hum Genet.* 2017;101(4):638. https://doi.org/10.1016/j.ajhg.2017.09 .006.

► For more than one group of authors—common in medical papers—separate them by a semicolon. Terms such as *for* or *and* are optional:

Singh AK, Szczech L, Tang KL, et al; for CHOIR Investigators. Correction of anemia with epoetin alfa in chronic kidney disease. *N Engl J Med.* 2006;355(20):2085–2098.

► AMA's use of period-free abbreviations extends to many terms, including "et al"—in which "et" is a word and "al" is an abbreviation. (Most publications would write it "et al."—with a period.)

Abstract of article

Erkut S, Uckan S. Alveolar distraction osteogenesis and implant placement in a severely resorbed maxilla: a clini-cal report [abstract]. *J Prosthet Dent.* 2006;95(5):340–343.

Erkut S, Uckan S. Alveolar distraction osteogenesis and implant placement in a severely resorbed maxilla: a clini-cal report [abstract taken from *Dent Abstr.* 2007;52(1):17–19]. *J Prosthet Dent.* 2006;95(5):340–343.

► The upper reference is to the abstract, as published in the article itself. The lower reference is to the same abstract, pub-lished in a different journal.

Preprint or unpublished paper	Song Z. Using Medicare prices—toward equity and affordability in the ACA marketplace. [Epub ahead of print October 18, 2017]. *N Engl J Med.* https://doi.org/10.1056/ NEJMp1710020. ▸ Once the journal has been published, information about issue and pagination should be added to the citation. Flynn HW. Management options for vitreomacular traction: use an individualized approach. Paper presented at: Retina Subspecialty Day, Annual Meeting of the American Academy of Ophthalmology; October 14, 2016; Chicago, IL.
Published letter, comment, or editorial	Guazzi M, Reina G. Regarding article, Aspirin use and outcomes in a community-based cohort of 7352 patients discharged after first hospitalization for heart failure [letter]. *Circulation.* 2007;115(4):e54. https://doi.org/10 .1161/CIRCULATIONAHA.106.646182. Baden LR, Rubin EJ, Morrissey S, Farrar JJ, Drazen JM. We can do better—improving outcomes in the midst of an emergency. [editorial]. *N Engl J Med.* 2017;377:1482–1484.
Book, one author	Basu S. *Modeling Public Health and Healthcare Systems.* New York, NY: Oxford University Press; 2017. ▸ Book titles use caps for main words. Articles use caps only for the first word in the article title. Wiggins CE. *A Concise Guide to Orthopaedic and Musculoskeletal Impairment Ratings.* Philadelphia, PA: Lippincott Williams & Wilkins; 2007. Lizza JP. *Potentiality: Metaphysical and Bioethical Dimensions.* Baltimore, MD: Johns Hopkins University Press; 2014. ▸ Note that states are included even after well-known cities.
Book, multiple authors	Schlossberg DL, Samuel R. *Antibiotics Manual: A Guide to Commonly Used Antibiotics.* Hoboken, NJ: John Wiley & Sons; 2017.
Book, multiple editions	Briggs GG, Freeman RK, Towers CV, Forinash AB. *Drugs in Pregnancy and Lactation: A Reference Guide to Fetal and Neonatal Risk.* 11th ed. Philadelphia, PA: Lippincott Williams & Wilkins; 2017.

Mazze R, Strock ES, Simonson GD, Bergenstal RM. *Staged Diabetes Management.* 2nd rev ed. Hoboken, NJ: John Wiley & Sons; 2007.

- ► The edition number appears between the book's title and the place of publication.
- ► For an unnumbered revised edition, use "Rev ed" (followed by a period) in place of the specific edition.

Book, multiple volumes	Cone D, Brice JH, Delbridge TR, Myers B. *Emergency Medical Services: Clinical Practice and Systems Oversight.* 2 vols. Hoboken, NJ: John Wiley & Sons; 2015.

- ► To cite only the second volume:

Cone D, Brice JH, Delbridge TR, Myers B. *Emergency Medical Services: Clinical Practice and Systems Oversight.* Vol 2. Hoboken, NJ: John Wiley & Sons; 2015.

- ► The abbreviation for "volume" does not have a period. AMA eliminates periods after abbreviations.
- ► If the volumes have individual titles separate from the collective title, you can also cite them using the author (or editor) of that volume, plus its title and publication date, followed by the series name and the volume within the series. You do not need to include the editor of the series.

Chorghade MS, ed. *Drug Development.* Hoboken, NJ: John Wiley & Sons; 2007. *Drug Discovery and Development*; vol 2.

Book, multiple editions, no author	*Dorland's Illustrated Medical Dictionary.* 32nd ed. Philadelphia, PA: Saunders; 2011. *Nursing 2018 Drug Handbook.* 38th ed. Philadelphia, PA: Lippincott Williams & Wilkins; 2017.

Book, edited	Hurlemann R, Grinevich V, eds. *Behavioral Pharmacology of Neuropeptides: Oxytocin.* New York, NY: Springer; 2018. Gravlee GP, Davis RF, Stammers AH, Ungerleider RM, eds. *Cardiopulmonary Bypass Principles and Practice.* 3rd ed. Philadelphia, PA: Lippincott Williams & Wilkins; 2007.

Chapter in edited book	Prinz J. Is the moral brain ever dispassionate? In: Decety J, Wheatley T. *The Moral Brain: A Multidisciplinary Perspective.* Cambridge, MA: MIT Press; 2015:51–68.

Book, online or e-book	Dalal AK. *Cultural Psychology of Health in India: Well-Being, Medicine and Traditional Health Care.* New Delhi, India: Sage; 2016. http://web.a.ebscohost.com/ehost/ ebookviewer/ebook/bmxlYmtfXzEyNTYzODZfXoFOo?sid= aad89e12-a6e0-494f-a52c-f7a4b4d7a72a@sessionmgr4006 &vid=o&format=EB&rid=1. Accessed October 26, 2017.
	Yefenof E, ed. *Innate and Adaptive Immunity in the Tumor Microenvironment* [Kindle edition]. Vol 1. New York, NY: Springer; 2008.
Government document	Global Task Force on Cholera Control. Ending cholera: a global roadmap to 2030. Geneva, Switzerland: World Health Organization; 2017.
	US Environmental Protection Agency, Office of Air and Radiation, Indoor Environments Division. *A Brief Guide to Mold, Moisture, and Your Home.* Washington (DC): Environmental Protection Agency; 2012. https://www.epa.gov/nscep. Modified September 2012. Accessed November 4, 2017. ▸ Use journal style for titles of articles, and book style for titles of longer works.
Personal communications	▸ Using AMA style, your reference list cannot include personal communications such as letters, emails, text messages, private discussions, or informal talks. Instead, cite those in the text.
DVD or online video	National Library of Medicine. *Changing the Face of Medicine* [DVD]. Washington, DC: Friends of the National Library of Medicine; 2004.
	Madara JL. Talk presented at: 2017 AMA annual meeting [video]. https://www.youtube.com/watch?v=d6 -6UCiH728. Posted June 10, 2017. Accessed October 29, 2017.
Database	RCSB Protein Data Bank. http://www.rcsb.org/pdb/home/ home.do. Accessed May 5, 2017.
	National Institutes of Health. Office of Dietary Supplements. Dietary Supplements Subset Database. http://ods.od.nih .gov/Health_Information/IBIDS.aspx. Accessed June 30, 2016.

National Center for Health Statistics. Tables of summary health statistics for the U.S. population. Atlanta, GA: Centers for Disease Control and Prevention; 2017. https://www.cdc.gov/nchs/nhis/shs/tables.htm. Updated January 24, 2017. Accessed October 26, 2017.

Vital Health Stat 10 (243). DHHS Pub No 2010-1571. Hyattsville, MD: National Center for Health Statistics (US Dept of Health and Human Services); 2009.

Website, webpage, or blog	Zika cases in the United States: Cumulative Zika virus disease case counts in the United States, 2015–2017. Centers for Disease Control and Prevention website. https://www.cdc.gov/zika/reporting/case-counts.html. Updated October 26, 2017. Accessed November 22, 2017. Sun R, Karaca Z, Wong HS. Characteristics of homeless individuals using emergency department services in 2014. US Department of Health and Human Services website. https://www.hcup-us.ahrq.gov/reports/statbriefs/sb229-Homeless-ED-Visits-2014.jsp. Updated October 2017. Accessed November 3, 2017. Lamberts R. There will be patients like this. Musings of a Distractible Mind. http://more-distractible.org/musings/2017/10/3/there-will-be-patients-like-this. Published October 2, 2017. Accessed October 21, 2017.
Podcast	Whitaker R. Muscle groups in the thigh [podcast]. Instant Anatomy. October 13, 2017. https://www.instantanatomy.net/podcasts/IA009.mp3. Accessed December 1, 2017.

To illustrate how these citations appear in the text, let's take the opening sentence of an article.

AMA: ILLUSTRATION OF REFERENCE LIST ORDER

Opening sentence	This research deals with the ABC transporter family and builds on prior studies by Nguyen et al,[1] Sheps et al,[2] and Kerr.[3]
Reference list (in order of appearance in text)	1. Nguyen VNT, Moon S, Jung, K. Molecular biology: Genome-wide expression analysis of rice ABC transporter family across spatio-temporal samples and in response to abiotic stresses. *J Plant Physiol.* 2014;171(14):1276–1288. 2. Sheps JA, Ralph S, Zhao Z, Baillie DL, Ling V. The ABC transporter gene family of *Caenorhabditis elegans* has implications for the evolutionary dynamics of multidrug resistance in eukaryotes. *Genome Biol.* 2004;5(3):R15. 3. Kerr ID. Sequence analysis of twin ATP binding cassette proteins involved in translational control, antibiotic resistance, and ribonuclease L inhibition. *Biochem Biophys Res Commun.* 2004;315(1):166–173. ▸ Nguyen's article is listed first because it is the first one mentioned in the text. Notice that "et al" does not include a period when it is used in sentences, according to AMA style.

Finally, all medical articles have an electronic identification number, known as a PMID. You are not required to include it, but it often helps your readers. It will help you, too, if you need to return to the article. If you include a PMID, you do not need to include a DOI or URL. The PMID appears as the last item in the citation and is followed by a period:

> Christakos S. In search of regulatory circuits that control the biological activity of vitamin D. *J Biol Chem.* 2017;292(42):17559–17560. PMID: 29055009.

The PMID identifies the document within the PubMed database, which includes virtually all biomedical journals. This database was developed at the National Library of Medicine, and it is available online at http://www.ncbi.nlm.nih.gov/pubmed/.

8 ACS CITATIONS FOR CHEMISTRY

The American Chemical Society (ACS) has its own style guide, *The ACS Style Guide: Effective Communication of Scientific Information*, 3rd ed. (Washington, DC: American Chemical Society, 2006). The guidelines for citations, which are also available online at the ACS's website, give you a choice of citation formats:

- In-text citations with name and year, similar to APA or CSE. The reference list is alphabetized and appears at the end of the paper.
- Numbered citations, with a reference list at the end of the paper. End references are numbered in the order they appear in the text. These numbered citations, as they appear in the text itself, are either
  - superscript, such as[23], or
  - parentheses with the number in italics, such as (*23*).

Each format is used by scores of chemistry journals. Your lab, instructor, or journal may prefer one over the other. Whichever one you choose, use it consistently throughout each paper.

Fortunately, you collect the same information for either format. In fact, the items in the reference list are presented exactly the same way whether the list is numbered or alphabetized. And both types of reference lists use hanging indents. That is, the first line of each reference is full length; all subsequent lines are indented.

As you'll see below, there are some format differences, particularly between citations for journal articles and books. For example, publication dates are boldface in journal citations but not in book citations. There is no explanation for these mysterious details. My guess: the chemists were overcome by fumes many years ago, and the odd results are now beloved traditions.

ACS (CHEMISTRY): REFERENCE LIST AND IN-TEXT CITATIONS

Journal article	Reference list	Schoepff, L.; Kocher, L.; Durot S.; Heitz, V. Chemically Induced Breathing of Flexible Porphyrinic Covalent Cages. *J. Org. Chem.* **2017,** *82,* 5845–5851.

▸ or

Schoepff, L.; Kocher, L.; Durot S.; Heitz, V. *J. Org. Chem.* **2017,** *82,* 5845–5851.

Xing, Y.; Lin, H.; Wang, F.; Lu, P. An Efficient D-A Dyad for Solvent Polarity Sensor. *Sens. Actuators, B* **2006,** *114,* 28–31.

▸ or

Xing, Y.; Lin, H.; Wang, F.; Lu, P. *Sens. Actuators, B* **2006,** *114,* 28–31.

▸ Authors' names are separated by semicolons.

▸ Articles title may be included or omitted. Just be consistent, of course. (Until recently, article titles were always omitted. Now the *ACS Style Guide* considers it "desirable" to include the title, both to indicate the subject matter and to help readers find it.) Words in the article title are capitalized as they would be in a book title.

▸ Journal titles are italicized and abbreviated according to the *Chemical Abstracts Service Source Index* (CASSI).

▸ Year of publication is in boldface; volume number is italicized; complete pagination is in regular type. Do not put "pp" before page numbers.

Fadaei, E.; Martin-Arroyo, M.; Tafazzoli M.; Gonzalez-Rodriguez, D. Thermodynamic and Kinetic Stabilities of G-Quadruplexes in Apolar Solvents. *Org. Lett.* [Online] **2017,** *19,* 460–463. https://doi.org/10 .1021/acs.orglett.6b03606 (accessed October 27, 2017).

▸ A URL based on a DOI (appended to https:// doi.org/) is preferable to another kind of URL.

	In-text	(Schoepff et al., 2017)

(Xing et al., 2006)

(Fadaei, 2017)

Chemical abstract	Reference list	Taneda, A.; Shimizu, T.; Kawazoe, Y. *J. Phys.: Condens. Matter* **2001**, *13* (16), L305–312 (Eng.); *Chem. Abstr.* **2001**, *134*, 372018a.

▶ This article by Taneda et al. was published in a journal and referenced in *Chemical Abstracts*. This citation shows a reference to both the full article and the abstract. The abstract always comes second and is separated from the article by a semicolon.

Taneda, A.; Shimizu, T.; Kawazoe, Y. *Chem. Abstr.* **2001**, *134*, 372018a.

▶ Same article but shown only as mentioned in *Chemical Abstracts*. It is better to refer to the full published article than to the abstract, but that requires you to actually examine the full article.

Chem. Abstr. **2001**, *134*, 372018a.

▶ This is the same article, referred to solely by its *Chemical Abstract* number. That number—*134*, 372018a—is the CAS accession number. The number *134* is the volume, and 372018a is the abstract number in the print version of *Chemical Abstracts*. These numbers also work with the CAS databases that have recently taken the place of the printed *Abstracts*.

▶ In editions of *Chemical Abstracts* prior to 1967, abstracts did not carry unique numbers. Instead they must be identified by column number and their position on the page. Abstract f, column 1167, can be cited as 1167f (or 1167*f*).

▶ It is usually better to include the authors, as in the previous references to Taneda et al.

In-text (Taneda et al., 2001)
(*Chem. Abstr.*, 2001)

Book, one author	Reference list	Bahadori, A. *Waste Management in the Chemical and Petroleum Industries*; John Wiley & Sons: Chichester, UK, 2014; pp 23–42.

▶ Always include and italicize book titles.
▶ Put the publisher's name before its location.

Book, one author (*continued*)		▸ Do not use boldface for the year of publication. ▸ Do include "pp" before the page numbers. Or, if you're citing a whole chapter, you can list Chapter 3 instead of the page range.
	In-text	(Bahadori, 2014)
Book, multiple authors	Reference list	Theodore, L.; Dupont, R. R.; Ganesan, K. *Unit Operations in Environmental Engineering*; John Wiley & Sons: Chichester, UK., 2017. ▸ What if there are many authors? The *ACS Style Guide* says to name them all. It also notes that some chemistry journals list only the first ten, followed by a semicolon and "et al."
	In-text	(Theodore et al., 2017) ▸ Include up to two names for in-text citations; for three or more use "et al." If there are two authors, use this form: (Theodore and Dupont, 2017)
Book, online	Reference list	Olovsson, I. *Wonders of Water: The Hydrogen Bond in Action* [Online]; World Scientific: Hackensack, NJ, 2017. http://www.world scientific.com/worldscibooks/10.1142/ 10684#t=toc (accessed November 10, 2017).
	In-text	(Olovsson, 2017)
Book, multiple editions	Reference list	Tro, N. J.; Vincent, J. J.; Livingston, E. J. *Laboratory Manual for Chemistry: A Molecular Approach*, 4th ed.; Pearson Education: Columbus, OH, 2017. ▸ For a revised edition, use "Rev. ed." instead of "4th ed."
	In-text	(Tro et al., 2017)
Book multiple editions, no author	Reference list	*Reagent Chemicals: Specifications and Procedures*, 11th ed.; American Chemical Society: Washington, DC, 2016.

		McGraw-Hill Encyclopedia of Science and Technology, 11th ed.; McGraw-Hill: New York, 2012; 20 vols.
	In-text	(*Reagent Chemicals*, 2016). (*McGraw-Hill*, 2012) ▶ To cite a particular volume: (*McGraw-Hill*, Vol. 6, 2012)
Book, multivolume	Reference list	*The Encyclopedia of Mass Spectrometry*; Gross, M. L.; Caprioli, R., Eds.; Elsevier Science: Oxford, 2007; Vol. 6. *Hyphenated Methods*; Niessen, W., Ed. Vol. 8. In *The Encyclopedia of Mass Spectrometry*; Gross, M. L.; Caprioli, R., Eds.; Elsevier Science: Oxford, 2007.
	In-text	(Gross and Caprioli, Vol. 6, 2007) (Niessen, Vol. 8, 2007)
Book, edited	Reference list	*Applications of Molecular Modeling to Challenges in Clean Energy*; Fitzgerald, G.; Govind, N., Eds.; American Chemical Society: Washington, DC, 2017. ▶ or Fitzgerald, G.; Govind, N., Eds.; *Applications of Molecular Modeling to Challenges in Clean Energy*; American Chemical Society: Washington, DC, 2017. ▶ If there are only editors and no authors, the editors' names can go either after or before the title. Putting them before the title will make it easier if you are using an alphabetized reference list.
	In-text	(Fitzgerald and Govind, 2017) ▶ For in-text references, editors' names are treated the same as authors'.
Chapter in edited book	Reference list	Kolosa, A.; Maciejowska, I. In *Chemistry Education and Sustainability in the Global Age*; Chiu, MH., et al., Eds.; Springer: New York, NY, 2013; pp 15–26. ▶ or

Chapter in edited book (*continued*)		Kolosa, A.; Maciejowska, I. Polish Education Reform and Resulting Change in the Process of Chemical Education. In *Chemistry Education and Sustainability in the Global Age*; Chiu, MH., et al., Eds.; Springer: New York, NY, 2013; pp 15–26.
		▸ You may include or omit the chapter title (which would be styled like the title of a journal article); just be consistent.
	In-text	(Kolosa and Maciejowska, 2013)
Conference paper	Reference list	Fleming, L. Ecological Public Health, Harmful Algal Blooms and Climate Change. Presented at the 17th International Conference on Harmful Algae, Santa Catarina, Brazil, October 2016; Keynote speech.
	In-text	(Fleming, 2016)
Reference work or encyclopedia	Reference list	*Ullman's Encyclopedia of Industrial Chemistry*, 7th ed. [Online]; John Wiley & Sons: Hoboken, NJ, 2014. https://doi.org/10.1002/14356007 (accessed September 16, 2017).
		Vaidya, R.; López, G.; Lopez, J. A. Nanotechnology (Molecular). *Van Nostrand's Encyclopedia of Chemistry* [Online]; John Wiley & Sons: Hoboken, NJ, 2005. http://www3.interscience.wiley.com/cgi-bin/mrwhome/110498369/HOME (accessed May 5, 2010).
	In-text	(*Ullman's Encyclopedia*, 2014)
Government document	Reference list	US Consumer Product Safety Commission. *School Chemistry Laboratory Safety Guide (October 2006)*; DHHS (NIOSH) Publication No. 2007-107; National Institute for Occupational Safety and Health: Cincinnati, OH, 2007.

Energy Department. Meeting of the Biomass Research and Development Technical Advisory Committee. *Fed. Regist* [Online] **2017**, *82* (205), 49538. https://www.gpo.gov/fdsys/pkg/FR-2017-10-25/pdf/2017-23156.pdf (accessed October 2, 2017).

National Emission Standards for Hazardous Air Pollutants for Source Categories from Oil and Natural Gas Production Facilities. *Fed. Regist.* 2007, *72* (1), 26–43.

▸ The *Federal Register* is treated like a journal.

	In-text	(US Consumer Product Safety Commission, 2007) (Energy Department, 2017)
Patent	Reference list	Adams, G. W.; Mullaney, J. S.; Oar, M. A. Hybrid Thermoplastic Gels and Their Methods of Making. US Patent 9,736,957, July 12, 2017. ▸ It is also acceptable to omit the name of the patent.
	In-text	(Adams et al., 2017)
Video	Reference list	Luceigh, B. A. *Chem TV: Organic Chemistry* 3.0 [CD-ROM]; Jones and Bartlett: Sudbury, MA, 2004. Davis, R. B. *Foundations of Organic Chemistry* [DVD]; The Great Courses: Chantilly, VA, 2014. Szydlo, A. *The Magic of Chemistry* [Online video]; The Royal Institution: London, UK, June 4, 2014. https://www.youtube.com/watch?v=og8lANs6zpQ (accessed June 15, 2017).
	In-text	(Luceigh, 2004) (Davis, 2014) (Szydlo, 2014)
Website or webpage	Reference list	Biochemical Periodic Tables. http://eawag-bbd.ethz.ch/periodic/ (accessed August 10, 2017).

| Website or webpage (*continued*) | | ▶ If the page has an author, his or her name and initial appear before the title of the page: Oxtoby, J. Biochemical Periodic Tables. http:// . . . |
| | In-text | (Biochemical Periodic Tables, 2017) ▶ If no date of publication is included with a document on a website, use the access date for the in-text citation. |

9 PHYSICS, ASTROPHYSICS, AND ASTRONOMY CITATIONS

AIP CITATIONS IN PHYSICS

Physics citations are based on the *AIP Style Manual*, 4th ed. (New York: American Institute of Physics, 1990), and the more recent *AIP Physics Desk Reference*, 3rd ed. (New York: Springer-Verlag, 2003). Most physics journals use numbered citations in the text and the reference list. Items appear in the numbered reference list in the order they appear in the text.

The citations may be numbered either in superscript or in brackets, that is, as [99] or [99]. The *AIP Style Manual* uses superscripts, as do AIP's official journals, such as *Chaos* and *Low Temperature Physics*. On the other hand, the organization's own *AIP Physics Desk Reference* uses brackets, as do journals from the American Physical Society (APS), such as *Physical Review E*. Either approach is fine. Just be sure you use the same style for the text and reference list. (A few physics journals use the author-year style instead. It has an alphabetized reference list with hanging indents.)

Whichever format is used, individual items in the reference list look the same, at least for articles and preprints (which are the way researchers in this field communicate). References are brief: authors' names as they appear on the title page of the work (M. Shochet and S. Nagel), abbreviated journal title, **boldface number for the journal volume**, first page number of the article, and, finally, the year in parentheses.

AIP (PHYSICS): REFERENCE LIST

Journal article

[1] O. Budriga and V. Florescu, Euro. Phys. J. D **41**, 205 (2007).

[2] G. Battimelli, Nucl. Phys. B **256–257**, 74 (2014).

▶ The article's title is always omitted. Journal titles are abbreviated and not italicized.

▶ The publication volume (or issue number) and series are in boldface. For example, if a reference is to an article in *Physical Letters B*, issue number 466, page 415, then it appears as Phys. Lett. B **466**, 415 (1999).

[3] B. P. Williams and P. Lougovski, New J. Phys. **19**, 043003 (2017). <https://doi.org/10.1088/1367-2630/aa65de>.

Journal article (*continued*)	▸ This is an online-only journal; instead of page numbers, it assigns article numbers (in the case of the Williams and Lougovski article, 043003). ▸ The citation may also include a Digital Object Identifier (DOI); for the Williams and Lougovski article, it is 10.1088/1367-2630/aa65de. A URL based on a DOI (appended to https://doi.org/) is preferable to another kind of URL.
Preprint	[1] B. Schuetrumpf, W. Nazarewicz, preprint, arXiv:1710.00579 [nucl-th] (2017). <https://arxiv.org/pdf/1710.00579.pdf>. [2] F. Dai, et al., preprint, arXiv:1710.00076 [astro-ph] (2017). <https://arxiv.org/pdf/1710.00076.pdf>. To be published in AJ. [3] A. J. M. Medved, preprint, arXiv:hep-th/0301010v2 (2003). <http://arxiv.org/PS_cache/hep-th/pdf/0301/0301010v2 .pdf>. Published in High Energy Phys. **5,** 008 (2003). <https://doi.org/10.1088/1126-6708/2003/05/008>. ▸ A URL based on a DOI (appended to https://doi.org/) is preferable to another kind of URL. ▸ nucl-th = nuclear theory; astro-ph = astrophysics.
Book, one author	[1] Alexander Piel, *Plasma Physics: An Introduction to Laboratory, Space, and Fusion Plasmas* (Springer, Berlin, 2017).
Book, multiple authors	[1] Laurent Baulieu, John Iliopoulos, and Roland Seneor, *From Classical to Quantum Fields* (Oxford University Press, Oxford, 2017). ▸ The *AIP Style Manual* says to list up to three authors. If there are more authors, name only the first and add "*et al.*" in italics. Example: Laurent Baulieu, *et al., From Classical to Quantum . . .*
Book, multiple editions	[1] J. J. Sakurai and Jim Napolitano, *Modern Quantum Mechanics*, 2nd ed. (Cambridge University Press, New York, 2017).
Book, multivolume	[1] J.-P. Françoise, G. L. Naber, and T. S. Tsun, editors, *Encyclopedia of Mathematical Physics*, 5 vols. (Academic Press / Elsevier, San Diego, CA, 2006).
Book, edited	[1] Yatendra S. Chaudhary, editor, *Solar Fuel Generation* (CRC Press / Taylor & Francis, Boca Raton, FL, 2017).

Chapter in book	[1] Heinz Georg Schuster, in *Collective Dynamics of Nonlinear and Disordered Systems,* edited by G. Radons, W. Just, and P. Häussler (Springer, Berlin, 2005).
Database	[1] National Institutes of Standards and Technology, Physics Laboratory, Physical Reference Data. <http://physics.nist.gov/PhysRefData/>.

CITATION IN ASTROPHYSICS AND ASTRONOMY

Astronomy and astrophysics don't use the AIP/physics citation style or, for that matter, any single format. But most leading journals are fairly similar. They generally use (author-year) citations in the text, followed by an alphabetical reference list. The reference list follows some fairly common rules. It generally

- uses hanging indents
- contains no bold or italics
- uses authors' initials rather than their first names
- joins coauthors' names with an ampersand, &
- puts the publication date immediately after the author's name (with no comma between the name and date)
- omits the titles of articles
- includes titles for books and gives publisher information
- abbreviates journal names, often reducing them to a couple of initials
- lists only the first page of an article
- ends references without a period

Because there's no published style manual for astronomy and astrophysics, citation formats vary. I've standardized them based on the most common forms in the leading journals. Here are some illustrations, based on *Astronomy and Astrophysics* and the *Astrophysical Journal,* with a little tweaking for consistency.

ASTRONOMY AND ASTROPHYSICS REFERENCE LISTS

Journal article

Saffe, C., et al. 2017, A&A, 604, L4
Koepferil, C. M., & Robitaille, T. P. 2017, 849, 4
Stroman, T., Pohl, M., & Niemiec, J. 2009, ApJ, 706, 38
Khomenko, E., & Collados, M. 2009, A&A 506, L5, https://doi
.org/10.1051/0004-6361/200913030

➤ *All* astronomy, astrophysics, and physics articles are online and available through standard scientific databases. Adding the Digital Object Identifier (DOI) or other search information may help your readers find them more easily. A URL based on a DOI (appended to https://doi.org/) is preferable to another type of URL.

Journal article, several by same authors

Panaitescu, A. 2005a, MNRAS, 363, 1409
Panaitescu, A. 2005b, MNRAS, 362, 921
Pe'er, A., Long, K., & Piergiorgio, C. 2017, ApJ, 846, 54
Pe'er, A., & Ryde, F. 2017, IJMPD, 26, 1730018-296. 2006, ApJ, 653, 454

➤ The two articles by Panaitescu are listed as 2005a and 2005b because they have the same author.
➤ The two articles by Pe'er are *not* listed as 2017a and 2017b because they do not have identical coauthors.

Preprint

Kuruvilla, J., & Porciani, C. 2017, preprint, arXiv:1710.09379 [astro-ph]

Book, one author

Hoyle, F. 2015, Home Is Where the Wind Blows: Chapters from a Cosmologist's Life (Sausalito, CA: University Science Books)
Harwit, M. 2006, Astrophysical Concepts (New York: Springer Science)

Book, multiple authors

Mathur, R. B., Singh, B. P., Pande, S. 2017, Carbon Nano-materials: Synthesis, Structure, Properties and Applications. (Boca Raton, FL: CRC Press / Taylor & Francis)

Chapter in edited book

Thomas, J. 2012, in Solar and Astrophysical Magnetohydro-dynamic Flows, ed. K. Tsinganos (Dordrecht, Netherlands: Kluwer Academic), 39

Book in a series

Branch, D., Wheeler, J.C. 2017, Supernova Explosions (Berlin: Springer), Astronomy and Astrophysics Library Series

Chapter in a book in a series	Daly, P. N. 2006, in Astronomical Data Analysis Software Systems XV, ed. C. Gabriel, C. Arviset, D. Ponz, & E. Solano (San Francisco: ASP), ASP Conf. Ser. 351, 4
Unpublished paper or dissertation	Kilbourne, H, et al. 2017, US CLIVAR Workshop Report, Rep. 2017-3, https://doi.org/10.5065/D6KP80KR Fiore, F., Guainazzi, M., & Grandi, P. 1999, Cookbook for BeppoSAX NFI Spectral Analysis, available from https://heasarc.gsfc.nasa.gov/docs/sax/abc/saxabc/saxabc.html Lee, E. J. 2017, Ph.D. Diss, University of California, Berkeley
Website	SkyView, the Internet's Virtual Telescope <http://skyview.gsfc.nasa.gov/>

Researchers in the physical sciences often cite unpublished research, usually conference papers or works in progress that will be published later. Known as preprints (or e-prints), these papers are at the cutting edge of the field and are collected in electronic document archives. Besides collections at major research institutions, there's a huge collection at arXiv.org (http://arxiv.org/), with mirror sites around the world. Papers are readily accessible and easy to download. What's hard—unless you are on the cutting edge of physics—is actually understanding their content!

Preprints in the arXiv collection are classified by field (physics, astrophysics, mathematics, quantitative biology, and so forth) and, within each field, by major subfields. Papers are submitted to the subfield archives and are numbered by their date of arrival. As with journal articles, the titles of preprints are omitted from citations. Here are some examples:

Biswarup, P. 2017, preprint, arXiv:1710.09634 [nucl-ex] <https://arxiv.org/abs/1710.09634>
Brax, P., Cespedes, S., Davis, A. 2017, preprint, arXiv:1710.09818 [astro-ph.CO]

or

Brax, P., Cespedes, S., Davis, A., 2017, preprint (arXiv:1710.09818 [astro-ph.CO])

The classification system is as simple as the papers are complex. Take the Brax et al. paper. It's in the astrophysics archive (astro-ph), under the subject category of cosmology and nongalactic astrophysics (CO), was submitted in 2017 (17), in October (10), and is the 9,818th paper submitted in its category that month. Hence 1710.09818 [astro-ph.CO].

For the Biswarup article I included the URL for the PDF version, but that's not essential. Professionals in the field know where to find arXiv preprints, either at the main archive or on mirror sites. It's sufficient to list the ID.

Preprints like these should be cited and included in your reference list, just like journal articles. Unpublished does not mean uncited.

10 MATHEMATICS, COMPUTER SCIENCE, AND ENGINEERING CITATIONS

MATHEMATICS AND COMPUTER SCIENCE

Papers in mathematics and computer science use a variety of citation styles. References in mathematics are usually generated by a document typesetting system called LaTeX, which can churn out a number of different styles. As the writer of a paper, you may not create your own references by hand, but you will still want to check them for accuracy.

In most cases, references in the text are given by bracketed numbers. They may be listed sequentially, beginning with [1], with a corresponding sequential reference list at the end of the paper. Or if the reference list is organized alphabetically by the author's last name, the first reference might be [23], referring to the twenty-third item in an alphabetical list at the end of the paper (for an author named Simpson), while the last reference in the article might be [2] (author named Biel). Specific pages are rarely mentioned, but if you need to, use this form: [23, p. 14].

A less common style uses abbreviations based on the author's last name and date of publication rather than bracketed numbers. So an article by Hirano and Porter, published in *Econometrica*, volume 77 (2009), would be cited in the text as something like [HiPo09] or perhaps [HP09] or maybe just [HP]. It's your choice. This abbreviation also appears in the reference list, identifying the entry for Hirano and Porter's article.

Most books and articles are classified by subfield and uniquely identified in the Mathematical Reviews (MR) Database. Whichever citation system you use, you can include this MR number as the last item in each reference, after the date or page numbers. The MR Database is searchable through the American Mathematical Society's website at http://www.ams .org/mr-database.

If the article you are citing is available online, mention the DOI (Digital Object Identifier) just before the MR number. If there is no MR number, the DOI appears last. Style the DOI as a URL, appended to https://doi.org/;

for example, if the DOI is 10.1515/jgth-2014-0041, use https://doi.org/10 .1515/jgth-2014-0041.

In the following tables I show a standardized mathematical citation form. Many math journals don't stick to one format. Some use numerical citations for one article and alphabetical for the next. To add to the fun, they'll use the same style differently in different articles. One might list the author as R. Zimmer. The very next article (using the same style) lists the author as Zimmer, R. If I kept looking, I'd probably find one that calls him Bob Zimmer. One article puts the publication date in parentheses; the next one doesn't. In one, the reference list uses italics for every article title and regular type for journal names. The next one does exactly the opposite. Some use boldface for journal numbers, and others don't. Frankly, I don't think any of this matters very much, as long as you are consistent and your professor or publisher is okay with it.

I've swept away these variations and idiosyncrasies. The tables below use consistent rules, based on recent editions of major journals in mathematics and computer science.

MATHEMATICS: NUMBERED REFERENCE LIST (ALPHABETICAL ORDER)

Journal article	[1] A. Obus, *The local lifting problem for A4*, Algebra Number Theory **10** (2016), pp. 1683–1693.
	[2] D. W. Smith and R. G. Sanfelice, *A hybrid feedback control strategy for autonomous waypoint transitioning and loitering of unmanned aerial vehicles*, Nonlinear Anal. Hybrid Syst. **26** (2017), pp. 115–136.
	[3] N. P. Strickland, *Gross-Hopkins duality*, Topology **39** (2000), pp. 1021–1033.
	[4] ——— , *Common subbundles and intersections of divisors*, Algebr. Geom. Topol. **2** (2002), pp. 1061–1118.

- ▸ Bracketed numbers go in the left margin. References are listed in numerical order, or in alphabetical order, by author's name. For each author in an alphabetical list, the articles or books are listed in their order of publication, with the earliest ones first.
- ▸ If an author's name is repeated (and there are no new coauthors), then use three em dashes, followed by a comma. (Em dashes are simply long dashes, about the length of the letter *m*. If for some reason you can't find these em dashes, just use three hyphens.)
- ▸ Journal titles are abbreviated but not italicized. A full list of journal abbreviations compiled by the American Mathematical Society is available at http://www.ams.org/msnhtml/serials.pdf.

[#] C. Banks, M. Elder, and G. A. Willis, *Simple groups of auto-morphisms of trees determined by their actions on finite subtrees*, J. Group Theory **18** (2015), 235–261. https://doi.org/10.1515/jgth-2014-0041. MR 3318536.

[#] M. Leonelli, E. Riccomagno, and J. Q. Smith, *A symbolic algebra for the computation of expected utilities in multiplicative influence diagrams*, Ann. Math Artif. Intell. **81** (2017), 273–313. https://doi.org/10.1007/s10472-017-9553-y.

Preprint

[#] J. Glänzel and R. Unger, *Clustering by optimal subsets to describe environment interdependences*, Technische Universität Chemnitz, Fakultät für Mathematik (Germany), preprint (2017-3). Available at https://www.tu-chemnitz.de/mathematik/preprint/2017/PREPRINT_03.pdf.

[#] S. Dasgupta and J. Voight, *Sylvester's Problem and Mock Heegner Points*, preprint (2017), submitted for publication. Available at https://people.ucsc.edu/~sdasgup2/Sylvester.pdf.

[#] L. Chen, *Algorithms for deforming and contracting simply connected discrete closed manifolds (III)*, preprint (2017). Available at https://arxiv.org/pdf/1710.09819.pdf.

[#] A. Hoque and K. Chakraborty, *Pell-type equations and class number of the maximal real subfield of a cyclotomic field*, preprint (2017), to appear in Ramanujan J. ArXiv:1710.09760 [math.NT].

[#] G. Lyubeznik, *On Switala's Matlis duality*, preprint (2017). arXiv: 1705.00021v1 [math.AC].

▶ In mathematics, as in physics, there's a large, easily accessible electronic archive of preprints available at arXiv. The math collection is at http://arxiv.org/archive/math. Either you can cite the entire URL for a preprint, as the reference above for Chen does, or you can simply list the arXiv archival number, as the references for Hogue and Lyubeznik do.

[#] X. Sun, *Singular structure of harmonic maps to trees*, preprint (2001), published as *Regularity of harmonic maps to trees*, Amer. J. Math. 125 (2003), pp. 737–771. MR1993740 (2004j:58014).

Other unpublished papers

[#] A. Iserles and S. P. Nørsett, *From high oscillation to rapid approximation II: Expansions in polyharmonic eigenfunctions*, DAMTP Tech. Rep. 2006/NA07. Department of Applied Mathematics and Theoretical Physics, University of Cambridge, Cambridge, UK, 2006. Available at http://www.damtp.cam.ac.uk/user/na/NA_papers/NA2006_07.pdf.

Other unpublished papers (*continued*)	[#] M. Fang, *Data enabled algorithms and analytics of material structural change informatics*, PhD diss, University of Memphis, 2017. [#] R. Viator, *Analysis of Maxwell's equations in passive layered media*, IMA postdoc seminar, Minneapolis, MN, 2017.
Book, one author	[#] D. Eisenbud, *The Geometry of Syzygies: A Second Course in Commutative Algebra and Algebraic Geometry*, e-book, Springer, New York, 2005. [#] D. Kondrashov, *Quantifying Life: A Symbiosis of Computation, Mathematics, and Biology*, e-book, University of Chicago Press, Chicago, 2016. [#] M. A. Parthasarathy, *Practical Software Estimation: Function Point Methods for Insourced and Outsourced Projects*, Addison-Wesley Professional, Upper Saddle River, NJ, 2007. ▸ Book titles, unlike article or chapter titles, are capitalized headline-style.
Book, multiple authors	[#] A. M. Mathai and H. J. Haubold, *Linear Algebra: A Course for Physicists and Engineers*, Birkhäuser, Boston, 2017. ▸ If there are many authors, then name only the first and add "et al." Example: A. M. Mathai et al., *Linear Algebra . . .*
Book, multiple editions	[#] D. Hughes-Hallett et al., *Calculus: Single and Multivariable*, enhanced e-text, 7th ed., John Wiley & Sons, Hoboken, NJ, 2017. [#] B. Korte and J. Vygen, *Combinatorial Optimization: Theory and Algorithms*, 3rd ed., Springer-Verlag, Berlin, 2006. MR2171734 (2006d:90001).
Book, multivolume	[#] F. Dillen and L. C. A. Verstraelen (eds.), *Handbook of Differential Geometry*, vol. 2, Elsevier, Amsterdam, 2006. [#] D. Knuth, *The Art of Computer Programming*, 3rd ed., vol. 4, fasc. 3: *Generating All Combinations and Partitions*, Addison-Wesley Professional, Upper Saddle River, NJ, 2005. MR2251472. [#] J. Humpherys, T. J. Jarvis, and E. J. Evans, *Foundations of Applied Mathematics*, vol. 1, SIAM, Philadelphia, PA, 2017.
Book, edited	[#] B. J. Copeland, C. J. Posy, and O. Shagrir (eds.), *Computability: Turning, Gödel, Church, and Beyond*, MIT Press, Cambridge, 2013.

Book, translated	[#] P. G. Darvas, *Symmetry*, trans. by D. R. Evans, Springer, New York, 2007.
Chapter in edited book	[#] I. Boglaev, *Uniform convergent monotone iterates for non-linear parabolic reaction-diffusion systems*, in *Boundary and Interior Layers, Computational and Asymptotic Methods BAIL*, Z. Huang, M. Stynes, Z. Zhang, eds., Springer, New York, 2017, pp. 35–48. ▸ Notice that the chapter is capitalized like a sentence (i.e., only the first word and any proper nouns are capitalized), but the book title is capitalized headline-style.
Chapter in multivolume edited book	[#] W. E. Hart, *A stationary point convergence theory of evolutionary algorithms*, in *Foundations of Genetic Algorithms 4*, R. K. Belew and M. D. Vose, eds., Morgan Kaufmann, San Francisco, 1997, pp. 127–134.
Software	[#] T. G. Kolda et al., *APPSPACK (Asynchronous Parallel Pattern Search Package)*; ver. 5.0.1, 2007. Available at http://software.sandia.gov/appspack/version5.0/pageDownloads.html. [#] *Windows 10 Pro*, Microsoft, Redmond, WA, 2015. Available at https://www.microsoft.com/en-us/store/d/windows-10-pro/df77x4d43rkt/48DN. ▸ When there is no author, as with this Microsoft program, alphabetize by its title.

TEXT STYLE IN MATHEMATICS

Finally, all math papers (regardless of their citation format) have special rules governing the way to present standard terms such as theorems and proofs, as well as the way to present the text following these terms.

Mathematical term	Proper format for this term	Text after the term
theorem	THEOREM or Theorem	*Italicized*
lemma	LEMMA or Lemma	*Italicized*
corollary	COROLLARY or Corollary	*Italicized*
proof	*Proof*	Standard, no italics
definition	*Definition*	Standard, no italics
note	*Note*	Standard, no italics
remark	*Remark*	Standard, no italics
observation	*Observation*	Standard, no italics
example	*Example*	Standard, no italics

For more details, see Ellen Swanson, *Mathematics into Type*, updated by Arlene O'Sean and Antoinette Schleyer (Providence, RI: American Mathematical Society, 1999).

COMPUTER SCIENCE: CITING SOURCE CODE IN PROGRAMMING

Besides citing articles and texts, you should cite others' computer code and algorithms whenever you incorporate them in your own programs. Follow the same principles you do in papers: openly acknowledge the work of others, and tell your readers where they can find it. That can be done easily in the comment section. Say who wrote the code segment you are using, the version or date it was written, where to find it, and the date you incorporated it. Be clear about where the borrowed material begins and ends, and explain what changes, if any, you made to it.

There is one exception to this citation requirement. If an algorithm is common knowledge, you don't have to cite it.

IEEE CITATIONS IN ENGINEERING

Engineers use three citation formats. Some use APA, described in chapter 5. Most prefer a format designed by one of two professional associations, the Institute of Electrical and Electronics Engineers (IEEE, pronounced "*I* triple *E*") or the American Society of Civil Engineers. The citations in this section are based on the latest *IEEE Editorial Style Manual*, published online at http://www.ieee.org/. The next section explains ASCE citations.

The IEEE publishes hundreds of journals and conference proceedings, and not just in electrical engineering and electronics. It also publishes in computer science, bioengineering, civil engineering, aerospace engineering, and most of the other engineering disciplines. Still, if you're not sure IEEE is the style you should follow, consult your professor or teaching assistant.

Most IEEE journals use numbered citations in the text and the reference list. This system is similar to the one used in medicine (see chapter 7) and physics (see chapter 9). Items appear in the numbered reference list in the order they appear in the text, *not* in alphabetical order. Numbers in the text and in the reference list use brackets: [99]. The reference list uses a hanging indent to make it easier to find the numbers.

The numbers in text are treated just like any other information in brackets: according to Carmine [18]. To refer to more than one source, use commas or hyphens: in the earlier studies [3], [22]–[24]. Unlike other numbered systems, IEEE allows you to include a page number, a numbered equation, or other item along with the numbered reference: [23, pp. 18–23], [24, Fig. 13]. Equation numbers are usually in parentheses, no matter where they appear: [24, eq. (22)]. You should already know how to abbreviate page (*p.*, pl. *pp.*) and equation (*eq.*, pl. *eqs.*); for everything else, consult a dictionary. If you can't find an abbreviation, spell it out.

In the reference list itself, abbreviate authors' first names. If a reference has many authors, include them all. Capitalize titles of articles, papers, and the like as if they were sentences—only the first word and any proper nouns. Capitalize titles of books and periodicals headline-style. For journal titles, use abbreviations. For IEEE publications, you can find most of these abbreviations in the *IEEE Editorial Style Manual*. For anything else, consult the PubMed journals database available at http://www.ncbi.nlm .nih.gov/journals.

IEEE (ENGINEERING): REFERENCE LIST

Journal article

[1] B. Komarath, J. Sarma, and S. Sawlani. "Pebbling meets coloring: Reversible pebble game on trees," *JCSS*, vol. 91, pp. 33–41, Feb. 2018, https://doi.org/10.1016/j.jcss.2017.07.009.

[2] M. Inui and N. Umezu, "Quad pillars and delta pillars: Algorithms for converting dexel models to polyhedral models," *J. Comput. Inf. Sci. Eng.*, vol. 17, no. 3, 031001, Feb. 2017, https://doi.org/10.1115/1.4034737.

▸ Use abbreviations for number, volume, page, and month (except for May, June, and July, which are spelled out).

▸ IEEE prefers listing the month of publication rather than the issue number, if possible; you can also drop the issue number for consecutively paginated volumes (i.e., most journals in the sciences). But it's always okay to include it.

▸ Some online-only articles will not have page numbers. In the Samper et al. example, 041005 is the "citation identifier" used by the *Journal of Computing and Information Science in Engineering* in place of page numbers.

▸ For citing online sources, the IEEE follows APA. If a DOI is available—even if you read the article on paper—include it. If you don't see a DOI, list the URL (usually the address in your browser's location bar) instead.

Unpublished article or paper	[#] J. Yu, "Photonics-assisted millimeter-wave wireless communication," *IEEE J. Quantum Electron.*, to be published. https://doi.org/10.1109/JQE.2017.2765742.
	► If an article has been accepted for publication, use "to be published." If it has been submitted but not yet accepted, omit the name of any journal and say "submitted for publication" following the title of the unpublished article.
	[#] M. Cole, "Advanced nanoengineering towards the electronics for tomorrow," presented at the 12th Int. Conf. on Surfaces, Coatings and Nanostructured Materials (NANOSMAT), Paris, France, Sept. 2017.
	► Abbreviate *conference* and words like *national* or *international*, but for the most part spell out the name of the event.
Published conference proceedings	[#] L. Xie and Z. Mo, "Decision system of urban rail transit line conference construction sequence," in *Proc. 2nd Int. Conf. Transportation Engineering*, Chengdu, China, July 25–27, 2009, pp. 820–825.
	► The IEEE manual insists on page numbers.
	► The manual also lists a few terms to abbreviate, including those above. The full title for the proceedings in the example is *Proceedings of the Second International Conference on Transportation Engineering* (notice that prepositions and articles drop out).
Book, one author	[#] S. W. Ellingson, *Radio Systems Engineering*. Cambridge, UK: Cambridge Univ. Press, 2016, p. 92.
	► Include page number(s) unless the citation is to the whole book.
Book, multiple authors	[#] L. T. Biegler, I. E. Grossmann, and A. W. Westerberg, *Systematic Methods of Chemical Process Design*. Upper Saddle River, NJ, USA: Prentice Hall, 1997.
	► IEEE says to list all authors. If this gets to be impractical, list only the first and add "et al." Example: L. T. Biegler et al., *Systematic Methods . . .*
Book, multiple editions	[#] G. Rizzoni and J. Kearns, *Principles and Applications of Electrical Engineering*, 2nd ed. Columbus, OH, USA: McGraw-Hill Education, 2016.

Book, multivolume	[#] M. Muste, et al., Eds., *Experimental Hydraulics: Methods, Instrumentation, Data Processing and Management*, 2 vols. Boca Raton, FL, USA: CRC Press / Taylor & Francis, 2017. ▸ IEEE capitalizes the abbreviations for *editor* (Ed.) and *editors* (Eds). They do seem to like their capital *Es*.
Chapter in book	[#] A. Wada, Y. Huang, and V. Bertero, "Innovative strategies in earthquake engineering," in *Earthquake Engineering: From Engineering Seismology to Performance-Based Engineering*, Y. Bozorgnia and V. Bertero, Eds. Boca Raton, FL, USA: CRC Press, 2004, pp. 637–675.
Book, online or e-book	[#] D. Haskell, A. Pillay, and C. Steinhorn, Eds., *Model Theory, Algebra, and Geometry* (MSRI Publications 39) [Online]. Available: http://www.msri.org/publications/books/Book39/contents.html. [#] D. Keith, *A Case for Climate Engineering*. Cambridge, MA, USA: MIT Press, 2013 [Kindle version]. ▸ For internet sources you might omit "Online," since that's clear from the URL. To cite a Kindle book or other electronic edition, put that in the brackets instead of "Online" (e.g., [Kindle version]).
Patent	[#] C. Entsfellner and H. Heuermann, "Vectorial network analyser," US Patent 9,801,082, October 24, 2017.

ASCE CITATIONS IN ENGINEERING

Unlike the IEEE, the American Society of Civil Engineers prefers the author-date style for its book and journal authors. This style is similar to APA (chapter 5). The differences are (what else?) in the details. A few of these details can be found on the ASCE website.

The author-date style uses an alphabetical reference list. Each entry in the reference list must be mentioned in the text, and vice versa. Let's start with a few examples:

Brenner, B. (2009a). *Bridginess: More of the civil engineering life*, ASCE Press, Reston, Va.

Brenner, B. (2009b). "Infrastructure at the end." *Leadersh. Manage. Eng.* 9(4), 205–206.

Brenner, B. (2015). *Too much information: Living the civil engineering life*, ASCE Press, Reston, Va., 60–64.

Compare these if you'd like with the examples at the beginning of chapter 5 (featuring the eminent author C. Lipson). Like APA, ASCE uses authors' initials and puts the date in parentheses. Titles by the same author are listed in chronological order; two titles by the same author in the same year are alphabetized by title and carry letters after the date.

Unlike APA, ASCE prefers quotation marks around article and chapter titles. And like most science publishers, it uses abbreviations for journal titles. Where to find these? If it's not listed along with the journal article, search the PubMed journals database available at http://www.ncbi.nlm.nih .gov/journals. (Just remember to add periods to the ends of abbreviated elements in the title.)

In text, cite the author and year, with no intervening comma: (Brenner 2009b). If you need to include a page number, use a comma; separate two references with a semicolon: (Brenner 2009a; Brenner 2015, p. 62). ASCE journals often differ in these details. Mainly you need to worry about being consistent. If you happen to be writing for a particular journal, look at a few recent articles in that journal and style your references accordingly. If you can't find a particular type of example and it isn't listed below, look at chapter 5 for a model and adapt that.

For the sake of comparison, the examples in the table that follows cite many of the same sources as those in the IEEE section above.

ASCE (ENGINEERING): REFERENCE LIST

Journal article	Komarath, B., Sarma, J., and Sawlani, S. (2018). "Pebbling meets coloring: Reversible pebble game on trees." *JCSS*. 91, 33–41, 10.1016/j.jcss.2017.07.009. Inui, M., and Umezu, N. (2017). "Quad pillars and delta pillars: Algorithms for converting dexel models to poly- hedral models." *J. Comput. Inf. Sci. Eng.* 17(3), 031001, 10.1115/1.4034737. ▸ ASCE wants you to list volume and issue number instead of month or season. ▸ Some online-only articles will not have page numbers. In the Inui and Umezu example, 031001 is the "citation identifier" used by the *Journal of Computing and Information Science in Engineering* in place of page numbers.

- The ASCE online guide for authors doesn't give much advice for citing online sources. Because its system is close to that of APA, follow APA (unless your professor says otherwise). If a DOI is available—even if you read the article on paper—include it. If you don't see a DOI, list the URL (usually the address in your browser's location bar) instead.

Unpublished article or paper

Yu, J. (2017). "Photonics-assisted millimeter-wave wireless communication." *IEEE J. Quantum Electron.*, in press. https://doi.org/10.1109/JQE.2017.2765742.

- In the references, list all authors. In text, if there are three or more, cite only the first, followed by "et al.": (Yu et al. 2017).
- The Yu article is an early access article, not yet published in its final form. If you cite the advance version, it's best to say so.
- ASCE advises against including unpublished articles, papers, reports, and the like in the reference list. But you can cite them in text: According to A. Stradivari (unpublished manuscript, January 2018) . . .

Published conference proceedings

Xie, L., and Mo, Z. (2009). "Decision system of urban rail transit line construction sequence." *Proc., 2nd Int. Conf. on Transportation Engineering*, Southwest Jiantong University, Chengdu, China, July 25–27, https://doi.org/10.1061/41039(345)136.

- Like IEEE, ASCE abbreviates titles of published proceedings. Unlike IEEE, it substitutes a comma for "of the" and doesn't object to the preposition *on*.
- These proceedings were also published as a book. To cite the same paper but from the book, you could list the publisher instead of the conference location—in this case, ASCE, Reston, Va. Then you'd include page numbers instead of a DOI.

Xie, L., and Mo, Z. (2009). "Decision system of urban rail transit line construction sequence." *Proc., 2nd Int. Conf. on Transportation Engineering*, ASCE, Reston, Va., 820–825.

Book, one author

Ellingson, S. W. (2016). *Radio systems engineering*, Cambridge Univ. Press, Cambridge, UK.

Book, multiple authors

Biegler, L. T., Grossmann, I. E., and Westerberg, A. W. (1997). *Systematic methods of chemical process design*, Prentice Hall, Upper Saddle River, N.J.

Book, multiple authors (*continued*)	▸ List all authors in the reference list. In text, if there are three or more, list the first and add "et al.": (Biegler et al. 1997).
Book, multiple editions	Rizzoni, G., and Kearns, J. (2016). *Principles and applications of electrical engineering*, 2nd ed., McGraw-Hill Education, Columbus, Ohio. ▸ ASCE recommends "traditional" state abbreviations rather than postal codes (e.g., Pa. rather than PA). There is no traditional abbreviation for Ohio. To find the right one, use a dictionary or consult *The Chicago Manual of Style*.
Book, multivolume	Muste, M., Aberle, J., Admiraal, D., Ettema, R., Garcia, M. H., Lyn, D., Nikora, V., Rennie, C., eds. (2017). *Experimental hydraulics: Methods, instrumentation, data processing and management*, 2 vols., CRC Press, Boca Raton, Fla.
Chapter in book	Wada, A., Huang, Y., and Bertero, V. (2004). "Innovative strategies in earthquake engineering." *Earthquake engineering: From engineering seismology to performance-based engineering*, Y. Bozorgnia and V. Bertero, eds., CRC Press, Boca Raton, Fla., 637–675.
Book, online or e-book	Haskell, D., Pillay, A., and Steinhorn, C., eds. (2000). *Model theory, algebra, and geometry* (Online), MSRI Publications 39, http://www.msri.org/publications/books/Book39/contents.html. Keith, D. (2013). *A Case for Climate Engineering* (Kindle version), MIT Press, Cambridge, Mass. ▸ For internet sources, you might omit "Online," since that's clear from the URL. To cite a Kindle book or other electronic edition, put that in the parentheses instead of "Online"—e.g., (Kindle version).
Patent	Entsfellner, C. and Heuermann, H. (2017). "Vectorial network analyser," US Patent 9,801,082, October 24.

11 FAQS ABOUT *ALL* REFERENCE STYLES

Do I need to cite everything I use in the paper?
Pretty much. Cite anything you rely on for data or authoritative opinions. Cite both quotes and paraphrases. Cite personal communications such as emails, text messages, interviews, or conversations with professors if you rely on them for your paper. If you rely heavily on any single source, make that clear, either with multiple citations or with somewhat fewer citations plus a clear statement that you are relying on a particular source for a particular topic.

There is one exception. Don't cite sources for facts that are well-known to your audience. It's overkill to cite any authorities for the signing of the Declaration of Independence on July 4, 1776. There will be time enough to footnote them when you start discussing the politics of the Continental Congress.

How many citations does a paper have, anyway?
It varies and there is no exact number, but a couple per page is common in well-researched papers. More is fine. If there are no citations for several pages in a row, something's probably wrong. Most likely you just forgot to include them. You need to go back and fix the problem.

How many different sources should I use?
That depends on how complicated your subject is, how intensively you've studied it, and how long your paper is. If it is a complex subject or one that is debated intensely, you'll need to reflect that with multiple sources— some to present facts, some to cover different sides of the issue. On the other hand, if it's a short paper on a straightforward topic, you might need only a couple of sources. If you are unsure, ask what your professor expects for your topic. While you're talking, you might also ask about the best sources to use.

In any case, don't base longer, more complex papers on two or three sources, even if they are very good ones. Your paper should be more than a gloss on others' work (unless it is specifically an analysis of that scholar's work). It should be an original work that stands on its own. Use a variety of sources and make sure they include a range of opinions on any controversial topic.

You certainly don't need to agree with all sides. You are not made of rubber. But at least for longer papers and hotly debated topics, you need to show that you have read different views, wrestled with varied ideas, and responded to the most important points.

By the way, your notes can be negative citations as well as positive. You are welcome to disagree openly with a source, or you can simply say, "For an alternative view, see . . ."

WHAT GOES IN A CITATION?

Can I include discussion or analysis in notes?
Yes, for most styles, *except in the sciences.* Footnotes or endnotes are fine spots to add brief insights that bear on your paper topic but would distract from your narrative if they were included in the text. Just remember that you still need to edit these discursive notes, just as you do the rest of your writing. And don't let them become a major focus of your writing effort. The text is the main event.

If you use in-text citations such as (Tarcov, 2017) and want to add some explanatory notes, you'll have to add them as a special set of citations. They are usually marked with a superscript number, such as (Tarcov, 2017).[3] In this case, note 3 would be the explanatory text.

If you are writing in the sciences and already using superscripts for the citation-sequence system, you're better off avoiding explanatory notes entirely. If you really need to include one or two, mark them with an asterisk or other symbol. In this system you cannot use numbered citations for anything except references.

Some styles, notably Chicago and MLA, use shortened titles in citations. What's the best way to shorten a title?
One standard way to shorten a title is to drop the initial article and any other needless words, including anything in the subtitle (following the colon). That is, focus on the key terms to identify the subject of the work. These aren't necessarily the first words in the title. And sometimes a title is already short and doesn't need to be shorter. So for example:

Long form	*Guardians of Language: The Grammarian and Society in Late*
	Antiquity
	How to Write a BA Thesis
	"Situating Kingship within an Embryonic Frame of Masculinity in
	Early India"
	"Autonomous Pigs"

Short form	*Guardians of Language*
	BA Thesis
	"Situating Kingship" or (depending on the topic of your paper)
	"Embryonic Frame of Masculinity"
	"Autonomous Pigs"

In the new MLA style, the rules are slightly different. To shorten a title in this style, include the first noun with any preceding adjectives. If the title does not begin with a noun phrase, just use the first word, as long as it's clear which item from the Works Cited list you're referencing. So for the examples above you would shorten thus:

Short form (MLA)	*Guardians*
	How
	"Situating"
	"Autonomous Pigs"

In the sciences, I'm supposed to abbreviate journal titles. Where do I find these abbreviations?
The easiest way is to look at the first page of the article you are citing. It usually includes the abbreviation and often the full citation for the article. You can also go to various websites assembled by reference librarians, listing journal abbreviations in many fields. One useful resource is "All That JAS: Journal Abbreviation Sources," compiled by Gerry McKiernan, science and technology librarian and bibliographer at Iowa State, and available at http://www.abbreviations.com/jas.asp. And there's always the National Library of Medicine's publicly accessible database of tens of thousands of journals, available at http://www.ncbi.nlm.nih.gov/journals—and by no means limited to medical titles.

What about citing a work I've found in someone else's notes? Do I need to cite the place where I discovered the work?
This issue comes up all the time because it's one of the most important ways we learn about other works and other ideas. Reading a book by E. L. Jones,

for example, you find an interesting citation to Adam Smith. As it turns out, you are more interested in Smith's point than in Jones's commentary, so you decide to cite Smith. That's fine—you can certainly cite Smith—but how should you handle it?

There's a choice. One way is to follow the paper trail from Jones's note to Adam Smith's text, read the relevant part, and simply cite it, with no reference at all to Jones. That's completely legitimate for books like Smith's that are well known in their field. You are likely to come across such works in your normal research, and you don't need to cite Jones as the guide who sent you there. To do that honestly, though, you have to go to Smith and read the relevant parts.

The rule is simple: *cite only texts you have actually used and would have found in the normal course of your research*, not obscure texts used by someone else or works you know about only secondhand. You don't have to read several hundred pages of Adam Smith. You do have to read the relevant pages in Smith—the ones you cite. Remember the basic principle: *when you say you did the work yourself, you actually did it.*

Alternatively, if you don't have time to read Smith yourself (or if the work is written in a language you cannot read), you can cite the text this way: "Smith, *Wealth of Nations*, 123, as discussed in Jones, *European Miracle*." Normally you don't need to cite the page in Jones, but you can if you wish. An in-text citation would look different but accomplish the same thing: (Smith 123, qtd. in Jones).

This alternative is completely honest too. You are referencing Smith's point but saying you found it in Jones. This follows another equally important principle: *when you rely on someone else's work, you cite it*. In this case you are relying on Jones, not Smith himself, as your source for Smith's point.

Follow the same rule if Jones leads you to a work that is unusual or obscure *to you*, a work you discovered only because Jones did the detailed research, found it, and told you about it. For example, one of Jones's citations is to a 1668 book by Paul Rycaut, titled *The Present State of the Ottoman Empire*. I'm not an expert on the Ottoman Empire and certainly would not have discovered that book myself. Frankly, I'd never even heard of it until Jones mentioned it. So I'd cite it as (Rycaut 54, cited in Jones). I can do that without going to the Rycaut book. On the other hand, if I were a student of Ottoman history and Jones had simply reminded me of Rycaut's work, I could cite it directly. To do that honestly, however, I would need to go to the Rycaut volume and read the relevant passage.

Some scholars, unfortunately, sneak around this practice. They don't give credit where credit is due. They simply cite Rycaut even if they've never heard of him before, or they cite Smith even if they haven't read the passage. One result (and it really happens!) could be that Jones made a mistake in his citation and the next scholar repeated the error. It's really a twofold blunder: an incorrect citation and a false assertion that the writer used Smith as a source.

The specific rules here are less important than the basic concepts:

- Cite only texts you found in the normal course of your research and have actually used.
- Cite all your sources openly and honestly.

Follow these and you'll do just fine.

BIBLIOGRAPHY (OR REFERENCE LIST)

Do I need to have a bibliography or reference list?
Yes, for all styles *except* complete Chicago notes. If you use complete Chicago citations, not the short versions, the first note for each item gives readers complete information, including the title and publisher, so you don't need a bibliography. (You are welcome to include a bibliography if you use Chicago style, but you don't have to, unless your professor requires it.)

All other styles require a bibliography or reference list (remember: essentially the same thing) for a simple reason. The notes themselves are too brief to provide full information on the sources.

Should my bibliography include the general background reading I did for the paper?
The answer depends on how much you relied on a particular reading and which reference style you use. MLA, APA, and science bibliographies include only the works you have actually cited. Chicago-style bibliographies are more flexible and can include works you haven't cited in a note.

My advice is this: If a work was really useful to you, then check to make sure you have acknowledged that debt somewhere with a citation. After you've cited it once, the work will appear in your bibliography regardless of which style you use. If a particular background reading wasn't important in your research, don't worry about citing it.

Does the bibliography raise any questions about my work?

Yes, readers will scan your bibliography to see what kinds of sources you used and whether they are the best ones. There are five problems to watch out for:

- old, out-of-date works
- bias in the overall bibliography
- omission of major works in your subject
- reliance on poor or weak sources
- excessive reliance on one or two sources

These are not really problems with the bibliography as such. They are problems with the text that become apparent when someone looks at the bibliography.

Old sources are great for some purposes but antiquated for others. Many consider Gibbon's *Decline and Fall of the Roman Empire* the greatest historical work ever written. But no one today would use it as a major secondary source on Rome or Byzantium. Too much impressive research has been completed in the two centuries since Gibbon wrote. So if you were writing about current views of Byzantium or ancient Rome, *Decline and Fall* would be out of date. Relying on it would cast a shadow on your research. On the other hand, if you were writing about great historical works, eighteenth-century perspectives, or changing views about Byzantium, using Gibbon would be perfectly appropriate, perhaps essential.

"Old" means different things in different fields. A work published ten or fifteen years ago might be reasonably current in history, literature, and some areas of mathematics, depending on how fast those fields are changing. For a discipline moving at warp speed like genetics, an article might be out of date within a year. A paper in molecular genetics filled with citations from 2010 or even 2015 would cast serious doubt on the entire project. Whatever your field, you should rely on the best works and make sure they have not been superseded by newer, better research.

Bias, omission of key works, and overreliance on a few sources reveal other problems.[1] Bias means you have looked at only one side of a multifaceted issue. Your bibliography might indicate bias if it lists readings on

---

1. Ralph Berry, *The Research Project: How to Write It* (London: Routledge, 2000), 108–9.

only one side of a contested issue. Omitting an authoritative work not only impoverishes your work but leaves readers wondering if you studied the topic carefully.

The remedy for all these problems is the same. For longer, more complex papers at least, you need to read a variety of major works in your subject and indicate that with citations.

However long (or short!) your paper, make sure your sources are considered solid and reliable. Your professors and teaching assistants can really help here. They know the literature and should be valuable guides.

QUOTATIONS

I am using a quotation that contains a second quote within it. How do I handle the citation?
Let's say your paper includes the following sentence:

> As Michael Mandelbaum observes, "the English writer G. K. Chesterton once said America is 'a country with the soul of a church.'"[99]

Of course you'll cite Mandelbaum, but do you need to cite *his* source for the Chesterton quote? No. It's not required. In some cases, however, your readers will benefit from a little extra information about the quote within a quote. You can easily do that in your footnote or endnote:

[99] Michael Mandelbaum, *Mission Failure: America and the World, 1993–2014* (Oxford: Oxford University Press, 2016), 9. The quote is a paraphrase from Chesterton's *What I Saw in America* (New York: Dodd, Mead, 1922).

I am quoting from some Spanish and French books and doing the translations myself. How should I handle the citations?
Just include the words "my translation" immediately after the quote or in the citation. You don't need to do this each time. After the first quotation, you can tell your readers that you are translating all quotes yourself. Then cite the foreign-language text you are using.

In some papers you might want to include quotes in both the original and translation. That's fine. Either the translation or the original can come first; the other follows in parentheses or brackets. For instance:

> In Madame Pompadour's famous phrase, "Après nous, le déluge" (After us, the flood). As it turned out, she was right.

ONLINE SOURCES

I was reading a blog and found some information I want to cite. But the blog is not the original source. It links to some website for the information. Which one should I cite?

It's best to cite the location where the information originated. In this case, that's the website rather than the blog. To cite the webpage honestly, however, you actually need to go there and check it out.

Unfortunately, you can't always find the original source. One blog links to another, which links to a third, and you can't figure out who in this daisy chain originated the information. What should you do then? First, if you cannot find the original source, cite the best source you have and note that it says the information originates elsewhere (or does not indicate its source for the information). "Blog A, based on information from website B." Second, if you cannot find the original source, be very careful about using the information at all. You don't have a good way to tell fact from urban legend.

These rules are similar to those for print sources: Cite the source that originates the information, not a secondary source, if you can. And remember that to cite any source directly, you *must* go there and check out the information firsthand. You cannot just copy a citation from someone else.

For online sources, do I need to include the date I accessed the material in my citation?

It depends. Some citation styles require an access date, but most do not. However, it's always a good idea to record the date you accessed the material in case you do need it. For example, if a website does not have an official date stating when it was published, posted, or most recently modified, you might need to include an access date to help establish at least some timeframe for when the material on the site was viewable. Check the examples in the relevant chapter. Some instructors might also require access dates even if the official style does not. It never hurts to ask.

I know what a URL is, but what is a DOI? How do I know which one to include? Do I ever include both?

A DOI is a Digital Object Identifier, part of an international system for identifying and exchanging intellectual property online. It is usually a string of numbers, such as 10.1086/681095. It should appear at or near the top of sources, like journal articles, that are part of this system.

The correct way to include a DOI in a citation is by adding https://doi

.org/ before the number. So for the DOI above, the citation should say: https://doi.org/10.1086/681095. This effectively makes the DOI into a URL. (This is a relatively new requirement, so some of the style guides do not yet include it, but I have added it in all the chapters here.) If you paste or type that full string into your browser, you will be taken immediately to the source—try it!

DOIs are generally preferable to other types of URLs in citations because they never change. That means anyone who wants to look at the source you're citing will be able to find it. As you've probably discovered, URLs can sometimes change or disappear, which makes your citations less useful. But most general websites, like Wikipedia or nytimes.com or YouTube, don't have (or don't list) DOIs, so you have to cite the URL.

If both are available, most citation styles now either recommend or at least allow DOIs in place of URLs. You don't need to include both in your citations. Check the relevant chapter for guidelines.

What about other online identifiers, like PMIDs?

PMIDs appear in many medical and biological journals. The abbreviation stands for PubMed Identifier. The PubMed database includes virtually all biomedical journals plus some preprints. It is available online at http://www.ncbi.nlm.nih.gov/pubmed/ and has a tutorial for new users. This invaluable database was developed by the National Center for Biotechnology Information at the National Library of Medicine.

Other specialized fields have their own electronic identifiers. Physics, for example, has arXiv, an extensive online archive with identifying numbers for preprints (prepublication articles), which classify them by subfield.

You are not required to list any of these electronic identifiers in your citations, but doing so may help you and your readers.

Tip on citing online sources: as you take notes, write down the
- URL or DOI for the website or webpage (copy and paste to avoid errors)
- name or description of the page or site
- date you accessed it

I've just explained the difference between URLs and DOIs (and other types of online identifiers). I also covered why it's a good idea to record access dates, even if you don't need to include them in your citations.

Writing the name or description of a website is useful because then if the URL changes (as they sometimes do), you still can find it by searching.

If sites are particularly useful, bookmark them. If you add several sites for a paper, create a new folder named for the paper and drop the URLs into that. A folder will gather the sites in a single location and keep them from getting lost in your long list of favorites.

Finally, whenever you cite something that looks as if it is likely to change or disappear from the internet sometime tomorrow or even next year, it is a good idea to print it out and save a copy of it. This holds for such things as blog posts, comments on social networking sites, articles in wikis, and even online news stories: anything that might be redesigned, deleted, discontinued, or subtly (or not so subtly) altered without notice. If you're citing something like the online version of an article in a scholarly journal, however, you probably don't need to save a copy. Most journals have pretty strict rules about making and posting revisions, and they usually do a good job of archiving past issues.

Aren't there citation management programs that can handle all these issues for me?

Yes and no. There are some well-known programs that can capture information from library catalogs and other online databases and format it for you in most of the citation styles covered in this book.

It sounds easy, but these programs have significant limitations. They work best with books and recent journal articles, where the source information is usually standardized and available for download. They are less helpful when you want to cite a source that's older or more unusual—perhaps a letter in a physical archive, a video on YouTube, a painting in a gallery, a text message, or an article in a long-defunct newspaper. There simply isn't a database with full information about these items.

These differences in source materials mean that citation software is most useful if you are mostly citing books and recent journals or if you're in the physical and biological sciences or the quantitative social sciences. It is less useful if your sources are more diverse and therefore less likely to be encoded in standard databases, as in the humanities and interpretative social sciences.

Let me fill in some details. Programs like EndNote, RefWorks, and Zotero allow you to build libraries of source citations and plug them directly into your papers. You can pick from a variety of citation styles, and you can easily change from one style to another. The programs are designed to work with standardized databases, although you can type in the information if it's not available online.

The good news is that these databases are increasingly common. Most library catalogs and other bibliographic databases are designed so you can download citations directly into the software, and more and more publishers are following suit with their online catalogs. But as with any new program, you'll need to spend some time learning the ins and outs.

This learning process may take longer in the humanities and social sciences, where the range of sources means you'll need to do some extra work. Instead of just pushing a button and downloading your data, you'll often need to pull up a blank record and enter the data from scratch. These records have a specific structure for entering data. You'll need to follow that structure, enter the information carefully, avoid typos, and use any punctuation required by the program. In one program I use, for instance, multiple authors must be separated by semicolons. Not commas. Semicolons.

Later, when you insert citations into your papers, it's wise to double-check the output and make sure it's accurate. That applies to the materials you've downloaded from databases too. If the original material was encoded incorrectly, the citations will show it. I know. I once printed out a citation for a recent edition of Plato's work. It said the editor was Plato's coauthor. Actually Plato did not have coauthors, and if he did, he would have had to wait twenty- five hundred years for this one. I returned to the software and restored Plato to his rightful place as a single (and singular) author.

Before you start using the software, it helps to know which citation style you'll be using for your papers. It's not essential, but it helps. You'll know what to enter for each type of source, and you'll know what you can skip (each record will have spaces for countless details). You might even be able to catch what the software has missed and fix it.

One final point. If you are using your university's citation software and plan to continue your studies, perhaps at another university, you should check with your university and learn about exporting your citation library. If your citation data is stored on the university's servers, you'll need to make arrangements to move it. After you spent all that time building your library, you'll want to keep it with you as you continue your education.

Over time, the software is sure to get better and better and the databases more comprehensive. But right now it's still a mixed bag.

THANKS

Special thanks in this edition go to Susannah Engstrom, for her painstaking research on updates to the citation styles and new source types and examples. Thanks as well to Russell David Harper, chief reviser of *The Chicago Manual of Style* and the citation chapters of Turabian, for his insights, and to Mary Laur at the University of Chicago Press for overseeing the process. From previous editions, I remain grateful to Jenni Fry, Janet Dodd, Karen J. Patrias, Peggy Robinson, Sharon Jennings, and Peggy Perkins for their advice on specific citation styles and issues.

INDEX

in AIP and astrophysics/astronomy
styles, 141–42, 144
in AMA style, 126–27
in AMS and mathematics styles,
148–49
in APA style, 91–94, 96–97
in Chicago style, 24–26
in CSE style, 116, 121
in IEEE and ASCE styles, 153,
156–57
in MLA style, 65–66

Koran, citation of the
in APA style, 98
in Chicago style, 34
in MLA style, 69

lectures, citation of
in APA style, 99
in Chicago style, 35–36, 44
in MLA style, 69–70
letters (published), citation of in AMA
style, 128

magazine articles, citation of
in APA style, 94
in Chicago style, 26–27
in MLA style, 66–67
manuscript collections, citation of
in Chicago style, 30–32
in MLA style, 68
maps, citation of
in APA style, 101–2
in Chicago style, 42–43
in MLA style, 74–75
mathematics, citations in, 6, 147–52
medicine (field), citations in, 6, 126–32
MLA style, 4, 6–11, 57–83
musical sources, citation of
in APA style, 102–3
in Chicago style, 43–46
in MLA style, 75–77

names of authors and other creators,
rules for, 7–8, 10
in ACS style, 134, 135, 136, 137, 140
in AIP and astrophysics/astronomy
styles, 141, 142, 143
in AMA style, 126, 127
in AMS and mathematics styles,
147–48, 151
in APA style, 84–85, 87, 88, 89, 93,
100–101, 106, 109
in Chicago style, 18, 20, 23, 24, 25, 26,
34, 36, 38, 41, 48, 49, 51, 53, 56
in CSE style, 112–14, 116, 117, 118, 119,
121
in IEEE and ASCE styles, 153, 154,
157, 158
in MLA style, 58, 61, 62, 64–65, 66,
72, 73, 75–76, 79
newspaper articles, citation of
in APA style, 94
in Chicago style, 26–27
in MLA style, 66–67
notes, basic format of, 7–8, 160
in APA style, 84
in Chicago style, 15–16, 56
in MLA style, 59
numbers for in-text citations, basic
format of, 7–8, 160
in ACS style, 133
in AIP and astrophysics/astronomy
styles, 141
in AMA style, 126
in AMS and mathematics styles,
147–48
in CSE style, 112–14, 124–25
in IEEE and ASCE styles, 152–53
See also in-text citations, basic format
of
nursing, citations in, 6, 126–32

online sources, citation of. *See specific
types of sources by name*